LEADING ORGANIZATIONAL SUSTAINABILITY

Behaviors and Values to Master

Zuhair Hasan, Ph.D., P.E.

Pensiero Press

Leading Organizational Sustainability: Behaviors and Values to Master

https://www.linkedin.com/in/zack-zuhair-hasan-ph-d-p-e-leed-ap-42766b103/

Pensiero Press

Pensiero Press

http://www.PensieroPress.com

Books are available through Pensiero Press at special discounts for bulk purchases for the purpose of sales promotion, seminar attendance, or educational purposes. Special volumes can be created for specific purposes and to organizational specifications. Please contact us for further details.

Volume ISBN: [TO COME]

*Kindle and electronic versions available

Cover and interior: Gary Rosenberg • www.thebookcouple.com

10   9   8   7   6   5   4   3   2   1

CONTENTS

*I dedicate this book to my wife, Riham Karki,
who has been supportive, patient, and accommodating
throughout the entire process of my education.
I love you.*

*And I want to include my children, who waited patiently
for the completion of this book so I can spend more time
with them; Nada, Keenan, Neeshan, and Muhammad.
I am so grateful for your patience and understanding,
and I wish you will have a better and safer future.*

*Additionally, I want to include my father and first teacher,
Muhammad Hasan, and my mother, Khayriah Hasan,
for their continuous support and encouragement.*

I love you all; I am so blessed to have you in my life.

TESTIMONIALS

I am grateful for the opportunity to endorse *Leading Organizational Sustainability: Behaviors and Values to Master*, a captivating piece on management and leadership. Although the book is worth your time to read as an organizational leader, the book can also be read for personal leadership growth by anyone out there . . . I want to congratulate my friend, Zuhair Hassan, Ph.D. for the work well done in this piece.

Michael D. Kaluya, Ph.D., is a Professor of Economics and Department Chair Business Department, Tarrant County College, NE campus, TX and Author of best-selling book, *The Audacity to Change! Breaking the Berlin Wall in Africa.*

At the core of sustainable success is LEADERSHIP. Dr. Zuhair Hasan makes a compelling case for the refinement of systems and processes that serve as a catalyst for progress. Being a part of the solution where collaboration, compassion and courage intersect provides valuable insights into creating a triple win—our planet, people, and profits.

Dr. Debbie Phillips, CPM® is an entrepreneur, award-winning teacher and trusted advisor to CEOs and senior executives of diverse industries. In addition to her consulting, Dr. Phillips is an author and nationally acclaimed speaker on talent development, workforce strategies, and leadership. She has been recognized consecutively as a Woman of Influence and One of the Top 75 Women changing the face of the real estate industry. Most recently, Dr. Phillips received the J. Wallace Paletou Award from the Institute of Real Estate Management for significant contributions to the betterment of society as a whole through the role of a real estate manager. For more information, visit: http://www.TheQuadrillion.com

Organizational leaders responsible for transformation processes frequently lose legitimacy due to diverting interests and targets worldwide. What it needs to lead through a transformational period towards sustainability? What are the key behaviors and values to master the future development? The complexity of sustainability and the multitude of interactions make it a highly sensible multidimensional system where one changing factor can result in a transformation of the whole system. The investigations and publications as performed by Dr. Zuhair Hasan, summarized in his book *Leading Organizational Sustainability Behaviors and Values to Master* are highly welcome to enhance awareness of sustainability leadership and to segregate it against management. For the author, it is obvious that "leaders must exemplify appropriate behaviors of commitment to sustainability objectives." But how to lead organizational transformation to sustainability? In his book, Dr. Zuhair Hasan explains the essence of organizational leadership and sustainability and gives insights in practice, the day-to-day work and its impacts within and outside the organizations. "Leadership is a critical element in the process of planning, implementing, enabling, and driving sustainability." He demonstrates how organizational sustainability follows the organization's values and ethics and exemplifies how to engage internally and externally to trickle-down in the hierarchy and to involve all employees as well as clients into spreading sustainability. Private and public organizations at all scales need to reflect their future scope since sustainability will, at least as leading paradigm, determine the future of humankind. Transformation process will require leaders with adequate skills, knowledge, empathy and commitment to serve to the one planet of humankind—there is no other.

Dr. Engelbert Ruoss has more than 30 years' experience in teaching and implementing projects in the field of sustainability. He holds a Ph.D. degree in Biology from the University of Berne and a Master's degree in Museum Sciences from the University of Basel (Switzerland). As a board member of the Swiss Academy of Sciences and the National Commission for UNESCO he promoted sustainability in national and international organizations. His contributions to organizational sustainability include leading the Entlebuch UNESCO Biosphere Reserve Project. As the Director of the UNESCO Regional Bureau for Science and Culture in Europe and as the Organization's delegate to the UN Director's team he engaged in elaborating sustainability strategies and the SDGs, advancing the implementation of holistic development strategies primarily in UNESCO and joint UN programs in South and Southeast Europe. He is a lecturer in *World Heritage and Sustainable Tourism* at USI-Università della Svizzera Italiana, an advisor to managing territorial sustainability initiatives, and investigating and teaching in the field of governance and management of heritage destination's sustainable development.

Dr. Hasan hit a home run with this book! Through his many years of practical corporate experience, he strategically draws relevance between organizational success, generational significance, and leadership sustainability. The components of this book draw conclusions which would benefit any level of leadership progression. Leadership is starving for tools which will enable them to be more successful and ensure that organizations build longevity in these uncertain times. Dr. Hasan has successfully provided many of these concepts in his book and has offered leaders a method of sustaining positive leadership attributes.

Dr. Jeffrey Belsky is a professor at Northcentral University, a consultant at Solutions 21, and the author of *The Leadership Toolboxes.*

FOREWORD

by Dr. Elmer Hall

Dr. Zuhair Hasan brings together all the multifaceted aspects of a sustainable leader. At its heart, sustainability is quite simple. However, we have built economies and organizations that are not sustainable. So now we have organizations within a *built economy* that are change-resistant, and managers from top to bottom need to be transformational and lean into the sustainability effort. There was a simpler time when managers could often rely on one management style, say transactional, for line managers. But no more. The future sustainable leader needs to be like a superhero and this book show how all management to make progressive and purposeful steps forward.

Leading Organizational Sustainability: Behaviors and Values to Master provides a new model for a sustainable organization. Dr. Hasan delivers the first successful integrative approach starting with the four primary leadership styles. Through formal research, every leadership style used in this integrative approach is linked to sustainability leadership and management theory.

Leading Organizational Sustainability: Behaviors and Values to Master provides insights into the three dimensions of sustainability and unfolds the necessity for social sustainability in organizations. In addition, Dr. Hasan provides a comprehensive new definition of sustainability that goes beyond the needs and generational requirements.

At its heart, sustainability is about perpetual change, focused on long-term improvements. This book provides a new model for the organizational change process for organizational sustainability objectives. Additionally, it emphasizes the importance of organizational culture and provides insights into types of organizational culture and the characteristics of the sustainability-oriented culture. Furthermore, this book provides detailed information about efficient leadership and how this concept might be misunderstood in sustainability applications. Finally, it provides insight into trust leadership with emotional intelligence, which is critical to organizational sustainability.

Elmer Hall, DIBA, MBA, helps individuals and organizations plan for success that sustainably balances wellness and wealth. He holds several accredited degrees: a BA and MBA from the University of South Florida; and a Doctor of International Business Administration (DIBA) from Nova Southeastern University. For 25 years, he has taught at the undergraduate and graduate levels (MBA and MIS) at several Florida universities. He is a facilitator and dissertation Mentor for the University of Phoenix. His *real* education, however, is from his personal entrepreneurial ventures and those of his clients.

Dr. Elmer is the President of Strategic Business Planning Company (www.SBPlan.com), doing strategic consulting for startups and existing ventures. He has also been interim Sustainability Officer and Chair of a business incubator. Major clients: IBM, Ryder, NextEra (Florida Power & Light), and Burger King (Diageo).

Publications/Seminars are on survival/scenario, sustainability in business and education, innovation, economic development, patent planning, and Delphi Method research (ScenarioPlans.com, aka DelphiPlan.com).

In 2017, Robert 'Bob' M. Hinkelman, Dr. Elmer released the updates to their books: *Perpetual Innovation™: A Guide to Strategic Planning, Patent Commercialization and Enduring Competitive Advantage, Version 4.0* and the *Perpetual Innovation™: Patent Primer 4.0: Patents, the Great Equalizer of Our Time!*. SBP has developed the Commercialization of Patent Assets, COMPASS®, process for intellectual property (IP) management (www.IPplan.com).

Sustainability Blog: http://www.SustainZine.com

Intellectual Property & Innovation Blog:
http://www.IntellZine.com

To reach Dr. Elmer, please **e-mail**: DrElmer@SBPlan.com

ACKNOWLEDGMENTS

There are many scholars and professionals who have contributed to the success of this book. But I would like to specifically acknowledge the following for their support, understanding, and guidance which shaped my way to success, I am grateful for your advice and directions:

Dr. Cheryl Lentz

Dr. Elmer Hall

Dr. Michael Kaluya

Dr. Debbie Phillips

Dr. Engelbert Ruoss

Dr. Jeffrey Belsky

Mr. Gary Rosenberg

INTRODUCTION

After more than 30 years of the Brundtland Report, known as our common future, which described achieving sustainable development through economic growth, environmental protection, and social justice, we did not achieve a sustainable world. On the contrary, environmental problems are on the rise, unethical behaviors such as pay discrimination between genders, and financial exploitations in the workplace, continue to occur, tearing down social justice and harming the social fabric of societies around the world. Moreover, every few years, we hold our breaths during elections in different parts of the world as we realize that it takes only a self-centered, psychopath, short-sighted and power-hungry person to reach to the levels of power to be able to trigger a nuclear war and destroy life on Earth as we know it.

During my research for my dissertation, I was shocked to find out there were 10 animals that became extinct in the past 100 years, and there are 14 other animals that might become extinct in our lifetime, one of which is the Sumatran Tiger. What shocked me more was the world governments' spending on arms. In 2017 alone, governments spent close to $1.8 trillion on arms. It is estimated that it takes only one-tenth of that amount annually to eradicate poverty around the globe for 20 years.

On the other hand, we (worldwide) produce food sufficient food to feed us all. However, millions of people cannot meet their daily minimal nutritional needs because of poverty, and they do not have access to education, healthcare services, and shelter. Another shocking fact is that several nations around the world possess more nuclear warheads to destroy the Earth 20 times over. If we ask a simple question: how do we describe someone who keeps making the same mistakes over and repeatedly? The answer would be that we describe him or her as stupid or has mental problems. Therefore, I wonder if our (humans') collective intelligence is equivalent to *stupid* or *mentally disabled*. History teaches us that wars make everyone lose, and what do we do to learn from that? Instead, we do the opposite to logic and sound-thinking, as we arm ourselves more to destroy each other and all forms of life. I take this opportunity to call on all politicians to reconsider the need for weapons of mass destruction a million times. Why do we need biological, chemical, nuclear, and all other kinds and types of weapons? What will happen if the money we spend on weapons, instead, we spend on education, healthcare, helping others, and making life better? The world becomes a better place to live in and enjoy. And for those who think they are immune from the consequences of nuclear or other destructive wars, who might have built their underground bunker or underground city, I say what kind of life will you and your children be living? And who said that the consequences would not get you? For example, a nuclear war will make deep-water polluted for 1000 years and land polluted for a few generations, not to mention polluted air that will become unbeatable or deadly to breathe.

I can say that being the primary or most considerable power is a temporary illusion for those who are seeking power. It is like being a player in a soccer game with the ball under your feet, but the difference is that every player in the field is trying to have the ball, so if you keep it, you will get attacked, and if you give it away or share it you will be better off. If all players share the ball, then it is the best and ultimate situation, no one loses and instead of having a field of competition, it becomes a field of sharing and collaboration.

Once, I watched a video on the Internet where a Native American said, "We used to drink water from any river, but now they are so polluted that we cannot." So, we are no longer breathing healthy and clean air. On the contrary, 90% of the world's population is breathing polluted air. In 2019, India shut down schools twice and distributed breathing masks to school children in New Delhi due to smog and air pollution as they reached dangerous levels.

I have been raised in the Middle East, specifically in Palestine, an area torn up by wars, corruption, and poverty, and I always asked why world leaders do not fix these kinds of problems, until I realized that the world needs the *right* type of leaders; companies need the *right* type of leaders. We all need the *right* type of leaders in every organization who possess the suitable characteristics that enable them to successfully implement strategies that do not necessarily guarantee the continuation of our existence but at least will not accelerate or contribute to our extinction. We the people of Earth should not accept any more dishonest and corrupt politicians who seek our votes, but once elected, they turn against us and our interests. How is it ethical and legal for politicians to *work* for lobbyists against the health and welfare of the people who elected them? We should no longer accept to work for companies that do not respect us as value ends, and we should no longer accept anything less than sustaining solutions, products, services, and decisions.

The lack of the development of leadership theories, the mismatch between existing leadership styles, and challenges facing leaders such as sustainability and globalization cause misconduct of leaders, and their reliance on existing leadership styles, which cannot achieve organizational sustainability, and may not be practical for such complex issues. Consequently, incompetent, potentially unethical, and unfit leaders will continue to rise to levels of power, sustainability practices will continue to fail, such as financial scandals, economic distress, social injustice, and environmental problems will remain problematic. Therefore, there is a critical need for additional scholarship to secure a deeper understanding of leadership style for organizational sustainability, especially a style that emphasizes ethics and integrity and builds on them. Most organizations have adopted sustainability as their mainstream business, as we can see from electric cars, biodegradable products, the spread of solar and renewable energy usage, raising minimum wages, and generating satisfactory profits. However, the pressing question is why some organizational leaders are more successful in implementing and achieving organizational sustainability objectives than others. This book provides a clearer understanding of the type of leaders we need to achieve organizational sustainability objectives.

CHAPTER 1:
DEFINING ORGANIZATIONAL SUSTAINABILITY

Background

While sustainability has gained momentum among private business and government leaders, unfortunately, many others do not believe in it or do not consider it seriously. As a result, the human race is on the verge of extinction, our natural resources are depleting, and we are no longer breathing clean air. This chapter presents some notable milestones that contributed to the development and advancement of the concept and importance of sustainability, facts about gas emissions, consequences, and benefits of adopting sustainability strategies. Moreover, this chapter includes explanation of leadership for sustainability and the differences between management and leadership, and it defines sustainability and the concept of organizational sustainability.

Milestones in Advancing Sustainability Development

Sustainability is one of the most pressing and challenging issues facing organizations and their leaders in current times.

The concept of sustainability gained momentum after the Brundtland report in 1987 by the World Commission on Environment and Development (WCED, 1987), known as *Our Common Future* on sustainable development. In addition, the increased awareness of global warming, increased environmental disasters, increased poverty, and the spread of terrorism in the past two decades since 2001, increased the public interest in sustainability.

The United Nations (UN) conference on Sustainable Development held in Rio de Janeiro in 2012 put forth the path to eliminate poverty, protect the environment, and promote social justice. In 2015, the Paris Agreement (PA) was a radical commitment agreed to by 150 countries in addition to the European Union (EU) to tackle climate change (Bodle et al., 2016). The ultimate objective of the PA is to control a global average temperature below 2 Celsius degrees above the pre-industrial revolution level, with a goal of a 1.5 Celsius degrees limit (Bodle et al., 2016). Thus, the PA sets a long-term objective to control the average global temperature by limiting emissions caused by human activities. The PA is not a legal or binding agreement; however, the agreement calls for a leaders' duty, responsibility, values, and principles to respond and act upon these goals. Participating countries in the PA agreed to put forth measures to limit emissions. Therefore, companies also become aware of their responsibilities and should take decisions to respond to sustainability challenges (National Geographic, 2016).

Truly, sustainability is a common buzzword in business language and academic scholarship. It is a fair statement when we indicate that human survival is at risk since human activities have diminished half of the natural resources available in the world. Furthermore, population and consumption continue to increase. Organizations can play a positive role by becoming part of the solution instead of remaining part of the problem. Organizations have the financial capacity and human capital to contribute positively to sustainability advancement. In addition, organizations consume natural resources and affect the local and potentially the national economy by doing business. Economic development is based on interactions between humans and the environment or among humans. Therefore, these interactions must be based on sound values.

However, flawed practices by leaders of different organizations can lead to further exploitations of natural and human resources and might cause the failure of organizational sustainability programs. Therefore, conducting *business as usual* will not advance the achievement of sustainable world objectives.

Few Sustainability Facts

Leaders of different organizations should be aware of their organizations' energy consumption and emissions which adversely affect our environment. They should evaluate their energy usage and carbon footprint, whether in production, transportation, or facilities, to assess their conduct and possibly adjust their strategies to become more energy efficient organizations. In 2016, the carbon dioxide emissions from energy consumption in the United States were 5,170 Million Metric Tons (MMmt) (U.S. Energy Information Administration, 2018). The U.S. residents at the end of the same year, 2016, were 324,460,473 residents, excluding armed forces overseas (U.S. Census Bureau: National Population Totals and Components of Change: 2010-2019). Therefore, every individual's share in the United States of the emission generated in 2016 was 15.93 metric tons. Per the Environmental Protection Agency (EPA) carbon equivalencies calculator, this number of emissions can be sequestered by 18.8 acres of U.S. forests in 1 year (Environmental Protection Agency [EPA], 2018). Consequently, emissions of carbon dioxide from power generation plants, from manufacturing processes, or from transportations are significant contributors to global warming since they absorb heat reflected from Earth which otherwise would escape to space.

The productivity lost in metropolitan areas due to traffic congestions is estimated to be in billions of dollars annually, in addition to Green House Gas (GHG) emissions and their effects on the environment and the health of residents. Therefore, a sustainability program manager can endorse a telecommuting policy for the organization's employees, where each employee can work from home. In addition, sustainability managers should be aware of their responsibility to society and economic development. According to the Income and Poverty in the U.S. Report in 2016, there were 40.6 million people in poverty (U.S. Census Bureau, 2017).

Therefore, an organization investing in or adopting sustainability programs might have several reasons, including:

1. Reflection of its responsibility as a good world citizen.

2. It is considered a sound investment strategy and a competitive advantage.

3. Reflection of organizational values and fulfilling moral obligation.

4. Complying with regulations and laws.

One of the critical sustainability factors that caused the public to lose trust in financial organizations is the financial exploitations; corruption, fraud, and waste. Financial exploitation in organizations can cause several problems, including:

1. Reduce investment.

2. Reduce productivity.

3. Create income inequality and poverty.

4. Create a corrupt business environment.

5. Creates deterioration of values causing other adversary behaviors.

6. Negatively affect economic development.

Financial exploitations in any organization reflect adverse ethics and untrusted leaders, negatively affecting the organization's reputation. In addition, financial exploitations divert and waste money that leaders can use in many beneficial ways:

1. For developing human capabilities.

2. Funding beneficial projects and programs, developing more efficient processes and better-quality products.

3. Support charities; provide financial help to research and development.

4. To sponsor the poor and needy, and in many other positive ways to develop humans, nature, or the economy.

Sustainability strategies are numerous; however, their adoption and implementation reside in the hands of leaders who advocate and embrace sustainability. Therefore, leaders of organizational sustainability should be cognizant of their values, principles, and behaviors since everything they promote or demote has an effect on the success of organizational sustainability and on achieving sustainable world objectives. Organizational sustainability is structured on organizational values and ethics. Ethics are deeply rooted principles, and they guide our behaviors and perceptions of the world. Therefore, ethics should be a fundamental part of all business conducts at all phases. To become a sustaining business organization, they need transformation in many facets, such as changing consumers' behavior and increasing their awareness, reengineering production or service processes, supply chain, ecological footprint, and measurement tools.

Global Pandemic

The global pandemic C virus that has spread through the world in 2019 is known as The C virus. The World Health Organization (WHO) declared the C virus a pandemic in early 2020. The C virus outbreak started in December 2019 in Wuhan city in China; it continues to spread worldwide. Unfortunately, violence against women is prevalent. Research documented that violence against women increases during health emergencies, such as the C virus pandemic. Since we do not have satisfactory data about all world countries, WHO (2021) reported a substantial surge in domestic violence cases related to the C virus pandemic. Additionally, Takaku and Yokoyama (2020) indicated they found significant increases in the weight of children, social media usage, and mothers' anxiety because of the closure of schools.

While it is difficult to estimate the economic loss of any country because of the C virus pandemic, it has been estimated that each month of the crisis costs about 2.5-3% of the global GDP (Nuno, 2020). Overall, the global supply chains operation has been disturbed, affecting companies and economies across the world. Many people lost their jobs because of the C virus pandemic, and many companies, retailers, and restaurants to mention few, shut down their operations totally or partially in specific locations, and prices of consumer goods have surged in prices. Consequently, many consumers have also changed their consumption patterns, which resulted in unavailability of many goods around the world (Nuno, 2020). Additionally, the C virus influenced the way we perform in business. Many companies, educational schools and institutes, and government agencies have relied on the web to perform their functions. Therefore, those companies who prepared for crisis operations management and adopted telework policy in advance benefited from their experience. At the same time, those who were stiff and reluctant failed to adapt to the changing environment.

Leadership and Sustainability

Leadership is a critical element in the process of planning, implementing, enabling, and driving sustainability. Leaders' values and behaviors of business and government organizations are crucial in addressing sustainability challenges because leaders' values and patterns of behaviors of leaders form the capacity to create the required changes towards sustainability. Therefore, leaders must exemplify appropriate behaviors of commitment to sustainability objectives, including a financial exploitation-resistant culture.

Many organizations have been embracing and incorporating sustainability strategies successfully into their organizations, either because of their function, specific product, or they genuinely believe in sustainability. Such companies include the Seventh Generation company, specialized in environmentally-friendly home care products. Additionally, Patagonia, which makes its clothing from organic, recycled, or environmentally friendly material, and the EPA with a specific function of protecting human health and the environment. Other innovative companies that publicly adopted sustainability as part of their goals are Walmart, Nike, and IBM.

However, many corporate leaders remain hesitant to integrate sustainability into their organizational elements, as they do not understand what behaviors they need to master to achieve organizational sustainability objectives or lack of the driving values. Because there is inadequate research on practices that incorporate sustainability into organizational operations and integrating sustainability strategies into business, processes remains confusing.

Organizational sustainability is a challenging and a complex issue to contemporary managers; because it requires an optimization of social, environmental, and economic factors and because it is a multidisciplinary, multi-dimensional issue. Organizational sustainability does not reside in the hands of chemists alone, physicists alone, engineers alone, managers alone, or lawyers alone. Therefore, leadership for organizational sustainability is unique and different from other management or leadership styles.

Leadership for organizational sustainability needs special skills and abilities. Those leaders should be adaptive to change, can deal with complexity, engage teams, manage relationships, and manage emotions appropriately, requiring trusted leadership.

Leading organizational sustainability requires leadership and technical skills however, both skills are rarely found in one person. Hasan (2018) documented that previous research reveals that only 35% of employers encourage their managers to integrate sustainability into business operations and strategies, and not all employers understand sustainability, or they have misconceptions about it and are not aware of required talent and skills of their new hires. Therefore, it becomes critical to know what leadership behaviors, skills, and abilities necessary for successful organizational sustainability.

Leadership vs. Management

Many people mix *leadership* with *management* and are confused about the two terms. Some believe they are the same and mutually exclusive, and some believe they are distinct. Others believe leadership is part of management. Management can be a function of leaders, but leadership is not a function of managers. The only leadership style that matches management functions; in the author's opinion; is the transactional leadership style, and I explain this style in later chapters. A manager is concerned about results and controlling resources in meeting objectives. Managers assure that each employee has a clear and defined job description and acts and behaves according to policies and regulations within the hierarchy of the organization. In other words, leaders can manage, but managers are not leaders. The following elements formulate the concept and functions of management:

- Management is concerned with task accomplishment, and that is their focus; therefore, they plan, organize, and control resources for that purpose.

- Managers do not pay sufficient regard to the relationship with employees or subordinates since they rely on their authority and position of power within the organization to accomplish tasks.

- Managers focus on the efficient operation of their business unit through controlling resources, monitoring progress, cutting costs, and clear communication with subordinates to achieve tasks.

- Managers use punishment and reward (transaction) as a motivation to direct subordinates or employees to accomplish tasks. The reward can be the salary itself, bonus, or any other form of reward that is tied to performance.

- Managers avoid taking risks or disturbing the status quo of their organizations because they focus on short-term goals and focus on their own interests of keeping their position or moving up the hierarchical ladder within the organization by appealing to upper management. Most managers attain their position because of their technical expertise, business politics, or working hard.

Therefore, managers are guardians of organizational policies, standards, and guides. They rely on their technical skills, communication with subordinates, and on their authority and position of power to accomplish tasks. Managers do not encourage creativity or endorse innovation because they do not like to take risks and prefer a stable business environment.

On the other hand, leadership can be of formal hierarchical position or without since its essence is to influence others to accomplish agreed-upon goals, not only organizational goals. There are many leadership styles, and I will explain some of these styles in later chapters that I used in my research to reach the results presented in this book The following elements formulate the concept and functions of leadership:

- Leaders build relationships with followers, inspire them, care about their needs, and create and support changes. Leaders are role models to their followers and emphasize ethics and values in the workplace.

- Leaders tend to take risks because they trust their followers and have a strong vision to accomplish, and shared goals with their followers. Additionally, leaders encourage the creativity of their followers and allow for their contributions.

- Leaders motivate their followers by making them aware of the value of their contributions and by providing space for them to grow their careers. Additionally, leaders get close to their followers and become aware of their emotions and drives. Yet, leaders often keep a distance so they can make tough decisions when needed.

- Leaders consult with their followers before making decisions, or they share the decision-making with them. Leaders do not rely on their authority or position of power within the organization, but on the relationship strength they build with their followers to accomplish goals.

- Leaders plan for long-term results but maintain achieving short-term goals. Therefore, they invest in the development and education of their followers, and they invest in the reengineering and change of processes and new strategies.

From this review, a manager is concerned about results and controlling resources in meeting objectives. Managers assure that each employee has a clear and defined job description and acts and behaves according to policies and regulations within the hierarchy of the organization. When managers adhere to strict policies and guidance in managing their operations, they tend to be authoritative and maintain order, while leaders tend to create change and innovation. Managers do not encourage risk-taking as that can be considered outside the policies and beyond their authority. On the other hand, leaders encourage followers to take risks; and they welcome mistakes, which leads to innovation and creativity.

This book supports that leadership for organizational sustainability is not fully understood, and that operational leaders might not have established an understanding of their leadership style, specific or combination of behaviors essential to achieve organizational sustainability objectives. Therefore, the objective of this book is to enable operational leaders, specifically sustainability leaders, not to be left to rely on traditional leadership styles, instinct, or employ one specific leadership style. Traditional leadership styles are not sufficient to successfully achieve organizational sustainability objectives. This book provides operational managers with a prescriptive plan for managing organizational sustainability, and guidance to senior leaders and top executives to recruit and promote leaders to advance organizational sustainability. Additionally, this book provides insight for executive leaders in particular into the required training and development of operational leaders.

Defining Organizational Sustainability

As mentioned early in this chapter, one of the main barriers to adopting and implementing sustainability strategies into business units is the misconception of the sustainability concept. This barrier might be the number one factor in the failure of organizational sustainability. How do managers succeed in their roles towards sustainability if they do not grasp its true meaning? How could one define and evaluate the roles of governments, individuals, organizations and create measuring tools of organizational sustainability if one does not understand its true meaning? Therefore, understanding the meaning of sustainability is the first step towards building a solid foundation as everything revolves around this concept.

Metcalf and Benn (2013) highlighted the complexity of the sustainability concept, while Winston (2011) viewed sustainability as an ethical and moral obligation where he emphasized the link between social justice and the moral concept of exploitation. A sustaining organization can prove it can sustain profitability without engaging in practices and behavioral forms of unjust utilization of either human or natural capital (Winston, 2011). Organizational leaders should not set their goals to generate maximum profits. Satisfactory profits should be acceptable. This does not mean that more profits are not welcome; however, they should not be on the expense of the environment and/or of the health and welfare of all forms of life.

Sustainability

The most commonly used definition of sustainability is one defined by the UN as meeting the requirements or needs of the present generation without potentially risking the capacity of future generations to satisfy their requirements or needs (World Commission on Environment and Development [WCED], 1987). It is true that this definition considers *inter*-generational and *intra*-generational interests; however, let us take a closer look at this definition:

1. What is meant by the requirements or needs and requirements of the present generation?

The challenge is simple, as we do not know the needs of the current generation based on this definition. The needs of a Russian resident might be a better healthcare system, while a Syrian resident's needs might be security, and an American resident's needs might be better pay. How could we scale these intra-generational differences of needs to meet social justice criteria of equity? Shall we keep the pay of the American resident the same, since they might have shelter, quality food, education, water, and much more, so we can provide shelter to the poor in Africa or India since they might not have houses? What needs are we talking about? Survival needs based on Maslow's (1943) hierarchy of needs (as cited in Huitt, 2007) or more? The answer is we do not know the needs of the present generation meant by this definition, and there is no agreed upon universal social justice standard.

2. How could we possibly know the needs and requirements of future generations?

Similarly, we could not possibly know the needs of future generations. Airplane wings initially were made of wood; however, they are made from fibers now. Therefore, we do not know exactly what materials may be developed in the future.

Additionally, technology and inventions of new products advance at exponential rates; therefore, new materials can be explored and used. Morris (2012) indicated that sustainability concept was vaguely defined and could not be narrowed to protect or conserve natural resources because the needs of future generations were unpredictable due to technological advances, which in turn were unpredictable for future generations.

Thorium, a metallic element discovered in the early nineteenth century, is more abundant in nature than Uranium as a potential fuel solution to the world's energy challenges. Fossil fuels such as natural gas, coal, and oil, might not be needed in the future. Additionally, some countries do not depend on fossil fuels in their power generation, such as France. According to the World Nuclear Association (2018), France derives about 75% of its electric energy from nuclear plants, due to a long-standing policy based on energy security. The conclusion to draw is that we cannot predict the needs or requirements of future generations.

3. How does the environment and social justice fit in this definition?

Human needs depend on the environment and on the interactions among themselves. Therefore, economic development and social justice depend on these relationships. However, the UN's definition is human-centered and does not consider other species, centered only on human generations' needs. Therefore, other species and the environment are viewed as serving humans and not as independent and end values. Moreover, the UN's definition does not clearly address social justice since it focuses on undefined *needs*.

Consequently, what is the meaning of sustainability? As noted by Bateh et al. (2013), sustainability has fundamental integrated concepts such as *permanence* and *durability*, maintenance of its objectives over time, and moral responsibility of humans towards one another as well as towards the environment and other species. Therefore, sustainability is a value-driven condition or state; that must be maintained forever, where all forms of life can flourish. The first scholar who might have coined the meaning of sustainability as *flourishing* is Ehrenfeld (2005). Flourishing is an ideal state of the future that extends beyond life survival, with characteristics of self-actualized individuals, healthy livelihoods, thriving economy, human relationships, and environment (Schaefer et al., 2015).

Organizational Sustainability

From the preceding discussion on the concept of sustainability, it becomes clear that organizational sustainability is the positive contribution of an organization to the world's sustainability objectives; i.e., to the three tenets of sustainability; social justice, environmental protection, and economic development which are referred to as the Triple Bottom Line (TBL) of sustainability (Glavas & Mish, 2015). What I mean by *positive contribution* is not only not doing harm but also not allowing harm to occur or continue. Since doing no harm might be considered sustainable practice; however, not doing good should be considered unsustainable because not doing good can deepen harm.

For example, a company operating in the United States might be considered a sustaining organization by adhering to environmental regulations, generating profit, and complying with labor laws, and helping with student scholarships and philanthropic activities in the local economy where it operates, but yet there remains a famine or a disaster in another country where residents need food, medicine, or shelter to survive. By not contributing (given it is capable of doing so) food, medicine, or shelter to the residents of the other country, famine will turn into deaths, diseases will spread, or many people will become homeless in that country. Sustainability is not only a personal responsibility since corporations are likewise citizens of the world; therefore, they have a responsibility towards its sustainability.

Adherence and promotion of sustainability within an organization, government, or at the individual level is a choice that originates from one's values and beliefs. The behavioral choices that many organizational leaders are making now are beyond Earth's capacity to provide us with the required resources. Regulations, laws, and standards that regulate some behaviors to restrict harms to the environment, and social aspects of our lives, will not be able to dictate one's or organizational philanthropic policy, educating employees on certain topics, or recycling policy, or for one to take the bus to work instead of driving a private car (Hasan, 2018). Eventually, sustainability is based on the daily ethical and behavioral choices we make (Ehrenfeld, 2005). Especially when there is no consensus on a definition of sustainability and measuring tool (Montiel & Delgado-Ceballos, 2014). And because of the influence of the conflicting political environment about sustainability. Additionally, sustainability is a universal issue; where polluted air or polluted water can travel through the borders of countries, terrorism affects economies and the social life of many people throughout the world. Some environmental problems can extend through generations, through space and time. Ethical values that can be considered as an enabling framework for sustainability should be universal. Hence, sustainability within organizations requires value-based behaviors and actions.

A sustaining organization is one that preserves and justifies its existence financially and while doing so, contributes positively to human wellbeing and the environment. Sustaining organizations should promote social justice and fulfill their role in human development within and through their operations, which means any economic development actions that do not support the concept of sustainability are considered un-sustaining.

• The environmental tenet of organizational sustainability remains concerned with water use and pollution, material use and waste, gas emissions, and energy use.

• The social tenet of organizational sustainability includes concerns with employee satisfaction, employee wellbeing and development, philanthropy, human rights, and community relations, in addition to supplier and customer engagement.

• The economic tenet of organizational sustainability includes concerns with the financial performance of the organization, productivity, effectiveness of resources use, development, and acquiring new knowledge and talents.

Organizational sustainability might require the redesign of the organization to protect and renew environmental resources while developing the economy and to build the potential of people; capabilities, skills, and knowledge, to benefit the organization and humanity. Because some organizations might not be able to balance their contributions to the TBL equally or might not have the resources to contribute to any specific tenet of the TBL because of their type of business or because of other reasons; therefore, organizational sustainability can be defined as the integration and optimization of economic, social, and environmental strategies into the corporations' business units, operations, and relations, based on universal values and through cultural transformation to contribute positively to the world's sustainability objectives. When behavior is based on values, it can make the aspects of sustainability flourish and hence the lives on earth flourish. Hence, sustainability requires value-based behaviors and actions. Therefore, optimization is finding the best alternative among other alternatives.

For example, an energy company that generates electricity from burning coal might have acceptable financial performance, acceptable social programs through health, educational, and developmental programs for its employees; but its effect on the environment does not contribute positively to a thriving environment. Therefore, this energy company will have to perform analysis of sustainability measures and find the most effective alternative among the sustainability tenets; consequently, this company might have to increase its contributions towards social or environmental programs to reach an optimum state of organizational sustainability.

Social Tenet of Sustainability Ignored

Unfortunately, many organizational leaders focus on the economic and environmental aspects of sustainability, while social justice was and still remains ignored. Even though many company leaders embraced policies and strategies to reduce their organizational environmental footprint, they have done so to reduce costs of operation and for marketing purposes. Social sustainability or social justice is not only concerned with providing employees with a safe and healthy workspace, or diversity of workforce. In addition, organizational social justice should be about providing career security, managing employees' emotional distress, pay equality among genders, and building human capital. Social justice should factor in many other social consequences and elements. For example, instead of terminating employment of employees; leaders should look for other options such as developing employees' skills, reducing workload, and reduction in salary of all other employees to keep the entire workforce. The consequences of discontinuing the employment of a married employee can be devastating; it could lead to losing his or her house, divorce, financial stress, anxiety for the entire family, losing his or her car, or even turning to becoming an alcoholic, drug addict, or even criminal behavior.

Female pay continues to be lower than male pay of their counterparts, which is not only a shame on the forehead of employers, but also humiliating to women and a reflection of social injustice. According to the Income and Poverty report by the U.S. Census Bureau (U.S. Census Bureau, Report Number P60-263, 2017), in the United States, female to male pay ratio was 80% in 2017, while the median earnings for all male workers increased 3.0% and no significant increase for female workers from the previous year. While it is illegal to discriminate against female employees in the workplace by paying them less than their male counterparts, employers find loopholes in the law to get away with it, such as performance, seniority, and experience, or any other reason except sex-based reasons.

Equivalent pay for equivalent work does not mean one has

to do the same functions as another employee in the same company, but the functions, complexity of duties, responsibilities, and skill-set required must be equivalent. Probably, you have witnessed unjust promotions, bonuses, or salary increases for coworker counterparts that were doing the same or less complex tasks, or even functions that required lower levels of skill-set than what you were doing, which reflects unethical employer or manager, and social injustice.

Social justice in the workplace can be divided into two parts: *procedural* and *distributive* justice (Deschamps et al., 2016). Procedural justice is the fairness and impartiality of the process by which an organization distributes opportunities of hiring, promotions, and development, wealth; salaries; and bonuses, and privileges and rights among employees. Assume you are an executive manager and want to promote one of your subordinates to a management position. You design a recruitment process that includes collecting resumes, educational background of applicants, two interview phases, and you select the successful candidate which the interviewing committee recommends after they review all documents and conduct interviews with all applicants. That is considered a fair process. However, if you have announced the job opening date and closing date during a time period when one of your subordinates is on vacation and you never informed him or her by any means about the job, then that becomes unjust hiring. Many companies do not have procedural justice, and promotions are subject to management decision solely.

Distributive justice is the fairness of the process outcome. Managers can achieve job outcome fairness when an employee's job input and output are similar to someone else's, and they both have the same salary, bonus, and privileges. Other types of workplace justice documented by Deschamps et al. (2016) are *interactional* justice which focuses on the communication between leaders and followers. This type of justice can be embedded in either type of justice mentioned previously, procedural and distributive.

Healthcare benefits continue to be unavailable to many employees. *Unavailable* means that the healthcare benefits were not offered by employers to those employees. According to the Employee Benefits in The United States report by the Bureau of Labor Statistics (Bureau of Labor Statistics, USDL-18-1182, 2018), only 69% of private sector employees had healthcare benefits available to them. Small businesses that had 100 full-time employees or less offered healthcare benefits to only 55% of their employees, but employers with 50 full-time employees or less are not required to provide healthcare benefits to their employees; the money spent on healthcare benefits is most likely a tax credit. Healthcare and other benefits, including paid vacations or paid sick leave, help employers attract skilled employees and reflect care for their welfare.

Employers should provide a secure and safe working environment for their employees. Not only employers should maintain the security and safety of the facility from intruders or provide escape plan in case of fire, but they should also consider the safety and security of employees by eliminating workplace violence or injuries. As documented by the National Census of Fatal Occupational Injuries report by the Bureau of Labor Statistics (Bureau of Labor Statistics, USDL-18-1978, 2017), there were a total of 5,147 fatal work injuries in the United States in 2017, which included 2077 fatal injuries due to work-related transportation incidents, and 807 fatalities due to workplace violence. Taking good safety and security measures positively affects organizational reputation, ensures loss-prevention of organizational assets, and maintains the well-being of its employees.

As mentioned earlier, organizational sustainability is the positive contribution of the company or organization to the world's sustainability objectives, which extends to preventing or reducing harm from occur within its capacity. Reports indicate that The Republic of the Congo exports two-thirds of cobalt used in cell-phone batteries, computers, and electric cars. Researchers estimate that more than 30,000 children work in the cobalt mining in Congo under deadly conditions for less than $2 dollars per day. Since the cobalt prices are increasing due to the increased demand of electric cars, demand on cobalt is on the rise as well, causing misery to more children and declination of moral behaviors. Companies who import cobalt from the Congo can do many things to reduce or eliminate harming of children; (a) through their supply chain by demanding that children should not be part of the products they receive and (b) through their operations by recycling cobalt in old batteries. Companies using cobalt as their product can also contribute to the wellbeing of children in the Congo so no child will need to work.

Circular Economy

The concept of a circular economy has gained momentum in academic scholarship and attracted the attention of officials and many executives in organizations. Many scholars defined circular economy, but most of them agree that a circular economy is a recovering or regenerative system of natural resources input and waste which can be achieved by design and other process such as recycling and repair (i.e., Geissdoerferet et al., 2017; Kazancoglu et al., 2020). The concept of a circular economy considers natural resources to be limited and economic growth should reduce or eliminate its dependency on them, and that can be achieved by increasing material efficiency and value, reducing or eliminating waste in all phases of product use, and reducing the negative impacts on the environment. The concept of a circular economy created confusion among academics as well as practitioners where many confuse with the concept of sustainability and consider it as the solution to the world's sustainability issue.

A circular economy approach may be regarded as a prospective and necessary solution to some of the economic and environmental issues, but not the ultimate solution to the sustainability problem and should not be identified as or considered a replacement to sustainability. Sustainability leaders in organizations should be aware of the following notes on the concept of a circular economy so as to maintain their course on sustainability and not stray from the main problem:

- Leaders should be aware that efficiency of material use in manufacturing or in industrial processes is not sufficient if the product is not durable and reliable. Therefore, leaders adopting the circular economy approach should take into consideration not only the *recycling* of material, but also the durability and reliability of end products. The value of products should be increased and maintained for longer use.

- Leaders adopting the circular economy approach should adhere to the social dimension of sustainability and not view it as a by-product of the process and narrow it to be limited in the positive effects of the environment on humans.

- Leaders adopting a circular economy approach should provide solutions to the consumerism culture that is a major factor contributing to the sustainability problem.

- Leaders adopting a circular economy approach should address sufficiency in profitability for organizations since manufacturing or production of durable and reliable products will reduce the demands as well. Some industries can produce sound profitability; however, others can generate less profitability that traditional business models. Moreover, leaders should address a social dimension that can result from such an approach since fewer demands will result in termination of employees.

- Leaders adopting a circular economy approach should be collaborative, specifically with government organizations and policymakers so as to provide solutions for profitability and for the possibility of reducing employment in certain industries or business units.

A circular economy approach to economic growth has many benefits such as decreasing the depletion of natural resources, extended the life cycle of products, reducing the carbon footprint of many industries, and potentially increasing the gross domestic product (GDP). While a circular economy has social benefits, it is not a solution to the sustainability problem organizations and the world face. However, a circular economy is necessary to achieve sustainability (Geissdoerfer et al., 2015). Sustainability remains a more complex and challenging issue for leaders in all types of organizations since it focuses on the TBL and not only the economic factor.

QUESTIONS

1. Is sustainability important to you? Why? Why not?

2. What is your definition of sustainability?

3. In your opinion, why sustainability is important to your organization (if any)?

4. What behaviors and decisions do you experience at work or outside work that do not contribute to a sustainable world?

5. What is your leadership style for sustainability?

CHAPTER 2:
CHARACTERISTIC OF A SUSTAINING ORGANIZATION

Many organizational leaders successfully embrace sustainability initiatives into operations, policies, procedures, and external relations. Leaders of organizations experience pressure from the public as people's awareness of sustainability increases continuously, and the public expects organizations to do more for human welfare and the environment. Embracing sustainability social and environmental tenets into organizational operations and strategies can enable the organization to outperform its competitors (Eccles et al., 2012). While sustaining organizations differ from ordinary organizations in that their focus is only on profit, in many facets such as the business type, the location, or the financial capacity, sustaining organizations have many common characteristics, as discussed in this chapter.

Leadership Commitment

Leadership commitment is crucial to sustaining organizations as leaders, and top managers send the message of their sustainability objectives and commitment out to suppliers, customers, communities, competitors, stakeholders, and government officials, and down through the organizational hierarchy. Leaders are role models for employees to create organizational culture and policies for the organization, business units, and operations to support the long-term vision for sustainability. Leaders for sustaining organizations are different from leaders in traditional organizations (Eccles et al., 2012). Therefore, leaders of sustaining organizations demonstrate their commitment to sustainability in every action and decision they make, reflecting their vision and strategies in organizational design, structure, culture, and operations.

Leadership is essential for any organization seeking to nurture sustainability or adopt sustainability strategies into its policies, operations, and procedures and to possibly change its culture to infuse sustainability principles. Leadership is a fundamental element in developing and driving organizational sustainability, as indicated by many scholars (i.e., Elkington & Upward, 2016; Opoku et al., 2015; Suriyankietkaew, 2013). Leaders are responsible for implementing sustainability and creating needed changes to the organizational culture (Stuart, 2013). Therefore, leadership commitment to sustainability can be considered a driving force for successfully implementing and achieving sustainability objectives.

Leaders of organizational sustainability should demonstrate their commitment to sustainability as:

- They implement sustainability strategies throughout each business unit within an organization, including supply chain, production and operations, human resources (HR), communications, information technology (IT) support, and facilities.

- They use and create execution tools, where committed operational leaders translate sustainability goals into tools and execution programs for employees, suppliers, facilities, and other business units (Stoughton & Ludema, 2012).

- Leaders of organizational sustainability demonstrate their commitment to sustainability through products and services their companies provide.

- They adopt a long-term outlook of accomplishing objectives and generating lasting performance for their organizations.

- Their personal life demonstrates a commitment to sustainable world values and transforms their behaviors (transportation, purchasing, etc.) to become sustaining.

External Engagement

As world citizens, organizations do not exist in isolation from society and their environment, instead, they have responsibilities towards those environments and societies. It is difficult for one organization to deliver its products or services without engagement with other organizations. Therefore, external engagement is inevitable and important to involve and collaborate with stakeholders and other organizations to learn from, exchange ideas, and get feedback for the success of any sustaining strategy an organization adopts.

Additionally, external engagement includes developing and adopting sustainability best practices, though measuring or assessing tools and programs that emerge from collaboration with other organizations. Consequently, leadership should align business units, create a supportive culture, and possibly restructure the organization to meet sustainability goals. Swanson and Zhang (2012) suggested that implementing sustainability measures in an organization requires the review of organizational elements such as structure, measurement and reporting, culture, and planning. In some cases, leaders might have to create and implement a substantial change to foster sustainability within an organization.

Organizational sustainability leaders engage with suppliers and other consultants to create zero-waste products, zero-energy buildings, or zero-emissions processes through the supply chain management process. Additionally, leaders involve customers and communities for feedback and to address their concerns. In other words, external engagement is necessary to maximize the positive footprint of the organization through the three tenets of sustainability.

Internal Engagement

Executives decide organizational mission, policies, and goals; however, employees carry out goals and implement policies to achieve the mission. Hence, employees' commitment to execute sustaining strategies is important, requiring behavioral change and the employees' positive contribution to the organization's performance. Employees must realize the importance of their role and contributions to organizational sustainability; therefore, organizational leadership must create communication channels between different business units and promote innovation and employee-driven change towards sustainability. Moreover, leadership should emphasize changing employees' values to become responsible and accountable for executing sustainability objectives to create the required value-based organizational culture. Leaders can use the following strategies to increase employee engagement:

- Build relationships based on mutual respect, trust, transparency, and effective communication.

- Empower and encourage employees to be innovative.

- Provide employees with tools and the training necessary to perform their tasks.

- Clarify employees' responsibilities and leader's expectations.

- Provide continuous feedback and follow up on plans.

- Share success stories with other team members.

- Recognize successful accomplishments through the reward system.

- Maximize the efficient utilization of skills and talents.

- Balance workload among team members and their various levels of responsibilities.

- Utilize or develop a work-life balance.

Operational Excellence

Business organizations, through their operation, waste natural resources, cause the degradation of the environment, and exploit human capital, whether by transportation, manufacturing processes, use of energy, telecommunications, or other forms of business means. Additionally, business organizations face financial challenges of expenditure and profits and social issues, such as human capital management, development, and well-being. In addition, business leaders should manage through complex challenges in operation to maintain the existence and profitability of their organizations in the face of competitors. Therefore, the *operational excellence* (OE) concept resides in business processes' effectiveness and increasing operational efficiency (Ojah, 2015; Wojtkowiak & Cyplik, 2020) and continuous performance improvements to obtain a competitive edge (Moktadir et al., 2020). As a result, operational excellence can be viewed as optimizing business processes and systems including human and financial capital, information and knowledge system, equipment and tools, energy, and material (Wojtkowiak & Cyplik, 2020), facilities in addition to continuous improvements. One can infer that operational excellence is the continuous optimization of business inputs to achieve an optimal output.

Since OE combines efficiency with effectiveness, it extends its effect to customers' experience for long-term satisfaction and contributes to the organization's competitive advantage. Additionally, OE reduces production costs, material, and time and increases quality. Therefore, it becomes clear the contribution of OE to profitability, environmental development, and social justice, which in turn clarifies the relationship between OE and organizational sustainability. Moktadir et al. (2020) documented that to achieve sustainable development through operational excellence, all three dimensions of sustainability must be considered. Wojtkowiak and Cyplik (2020) performed a systematic literature review on OE and found a connection between OE and sustainable development.

Supporting Culture

One may consider organizational culture as a critical business facet to the success of any organization as culture can enable the promotion, fostering, and acceptance of any change, or it can hinder and demote innovation and change. Therefore, a supporting organizational sustainability culture is what leaders should strive to create and encourage. Organizational culture is best defined as the shared beliefs and values and shared understanding by which behavioral rules and norms can be judged to be accepted or not (Linnenluecke & Griffiths, 2010). Therefore, organizational culture can be regarded as the bedrock for organizations.

An organizational culture based on trust and supports innovation can enable transformational change required for sustainability (Eccles et al., 2012). In a seminal article, Ehrenfeld (2005) emphasized the role of cultural values in organizations as the fundamental element in creating sustainability. Some scholars considered culture in sustainability to be the fourth pillar of sustainability (Laine, 2016). However, culture is considered a necessary supporting element for sustainability but not a pillar throughout this book.

When organizational leaders create a culture based on shared values to support sustainability, employees become part of the implementation process and not resistant to sustainability initiatives, mandates, and strategies. When executive leadership demonstrates a commitment to sustainability, they create a vision and send a sustainability message through the organizational hierarchy to the individual employee, stakeholders, and the external business environment. For example, middle managers create strategic plans for their business unit. Furthermore, functional or operations managers translate strategic plans and vision into tools and programs of execution throughout their teams.

Therefore, organizational culture should be synchronized with the vision and strategic goals of the organization. The process of embracing sustainability into organizations can be viewed as a trickle-down effect from top management to individual employees (Stoughton & Ludema, 2012). Consequently, leaders should adopt and promote culture that supports and endorses sustainability.

Organizations can face challenges when leaders promote only one cultural value system because businesses ' external and internal environments are constantly changing, mainly because of globalization and the development of new technologies. Organizational culture can be considered normal when one value system becomes dominant over other value systems; however, overemphasis of one value system in organizations could be dysfunctional (Linnenluecke & Griffiths, 2010). The highlights of the sustainability cultural values within a sustaining organization can be summarized based on the level of adaptation as follows:

- HR level values include honesty, trust, fairness, empathy, commitment, effective communication, collaboration, sharing information, participative decision-making, and HR development.

- Process level values focus on productivity, quality, cost reduction, and speed of delivery, such as effectiveness, efficiency, flexibility, and responsiveness to market changes.

- Organizational-level values include stakeholders, governments, suppliers, and customers, such as transparency, adopting a long-term perspective of the organization, effective communication, collaboration, and humbleness.

The current organizational cultures of consumerism and economic growth do not support a sustainable world; actually, that is the cause of many of the unsustainable outcomes we notice around the globe, from economic distress to exhaustion of natural resources to accelerating poverty. This is not to say economic growth does not have benefits and life improvements. Prugh and Assadourian (2003) emphasized sustainability culture as a means to achieve universal human fulfillment potentially. Thus, a cultural transformation is needed from what is present now to a sustainable culture. Corruption and bribery can adversely affect the economic development of any country. We can find a correlation between higher levels of corruption and lower levels of economic development or economic swings in many countries around the world. Leaders should understand that ethical decisions and behaviors are not free, and they need courage and commitment. To hold onto values comes with a cost and a worth in many cases. Hence, ethical, cultural values need sacrifice with associated costs.

Mechanisms of Execution

Mechanisms of executing sustainability strategies, mandates, initiatives, and policies are the tools, programs, procedures, and processes an organization uses to translate its sustainability vision into reality. The practices that organizational leaders can use to execute their sustainability goals are vast; however, they include:

- Making sustainability objectives an essential part of organizational and employees' performance. Some organizational leaders might link achieving specific sustainability goals to team or employee performance and the reward system. For example, a company might have a goal for a product line manager to redesign the product to become a zero-waste product, support him / her with financial and human resources needed, and set an expected finish schedule. Therefore, once this goal is met, the manager; and possibly his / her team earn a performance award, while on the other hand, if they do not meet this goal, their performance rating lowers.

- Leaders adopting international or national standards on specific measures and making it mandatory for organizational members to meet those standards. For example, a company might choose to adopt the American Society of Heating and Refrigeration Engineers (ASHRAE) standard for energy efficient buildings. Winston (2011) suggested that a sustaining organization's practice should be assessed against global standards and not simply local standards.

- Leaders redesigning organizational production processes to make them fewer pollutants and more efficient.

- Leaders redesigning products and services to make them more environmentally friendly, of better quality, and meet social expectations (Clifton & Amran, 2011).

- Sharing prosperity and wealth with employees and extend that to needy communities or nations.

- Sharing knowledge and advancements with other organizations as well as other nations.

Reporting Organizational Sustainability Performance

Leaders for organizational sustainability need indicators to help them in assessing the sustainability progress or status of their organizations under various conditions. In addition, they need sustainability indicators to gauge and adopt sustainability strategies to help them attain a higher sustainability level with respect to sustainability indices. While there is no consent on a global sustainability index, a growing number of companies report their sustainability performance in the United States and Europe (Dilling, 2010). The following are two of the most used indices in measuring and reporting organizational sustainability development:

- The Global Reporting Initiative (GRI) is an international reporting organization located in Amsterdam in the Netherlands, leading sustainability reporting since 1997. The GRI organization pioneered corporate sustainability reporting since 1997. The GRI promotes sustainability and communicates the influence of organizations on vital sustainability issues to businesses organizations and governments. Companies from over 90 countries worldwide use the GRI standards in reporting their sustainability development.

- The Dow Jones Sustainability Index (DJSI) was initiated in 1999 to help investor companies become socially and environmentally responsible companies. Since Dow Jones has several sustainability indices, it has become the key reference on sustainability for companies and investors. The DJSI focuses on analyzing organizational economic, environmental and social performance, evaluating corporate governance, risk management, climate change mitigation, branding, supply chain standards, and labor practices. The trend is to encourage companies to operate in a sustainable and ethical manner.

Measuring and reporting organizational sustainability performance is a complex and challenging process. However, it is an important part of the overall organizational performance. For this reason, many companies create *Chief Sustainability Officer* (CSO) position to oversee this process and gather information and reports from all business units. Regardless of whether a company chooses to report its sustainability performance to any of the previous organizations, it is vital to generate a sustainability report for all stakeholders.

Supply Chain Management

The most critical element of leadership external engagement is supply chain management (SCM) since it is almost impossible for one organization to produce its products or services without obtaining parts in this process from suppliers. Therefore, managing this critical element of the organization is crucial to the success of implementing sustainability objectives. Leaders approach this part differently from traditional managers. Leading the supply chain management in sustaining organizations aims to reduce the harmful effects of the product or service, including its parts and sub-parts delivered to customers on the social and environmental elements of sustainability, generating a profit, and increasing the organization's competitive edge. Supply Chain Management for the purpose of sustainable development has been named by academics and practitioners as sustainable supply chain management (SSCM).

There are several reasons why organizations use SSCM, but the reasons include:

- Cost reduction, specifically when suppliers are from developing countries with lower labor and material costs. However, leaders of sustaining organizations must ensure that suppliers adhere to international standards such as international labor regulations.

- Organizations might not have financial capacity or capability to develop certain parts or processes internally. Some companies actually depend 100% on suppliers in developing their products; therefore, they only assemble parts and sub-parts from suppliers.

- To build a reputation. Some companies rely on the good reputation of certain parts to include them in their final product. For example, in early 2000, any computer that included an Intel processor was viewed as of high quality and better performance. Therefore, the Intel processor added value to the sale of computers.

- To access opportunities to advance their products. While many leaders in traditional organizations view supply chain as to shift or lower risks, sustainability leaders view it as an opportunity to develop sustainable products. (See Figure 1 on the following page.)

Characteristics of Sustainable Supply Chain

It becomes obvious that a sustainable supply chain plays a critical role in the development and determination of organizational strategies and structure towards achieving sustainability

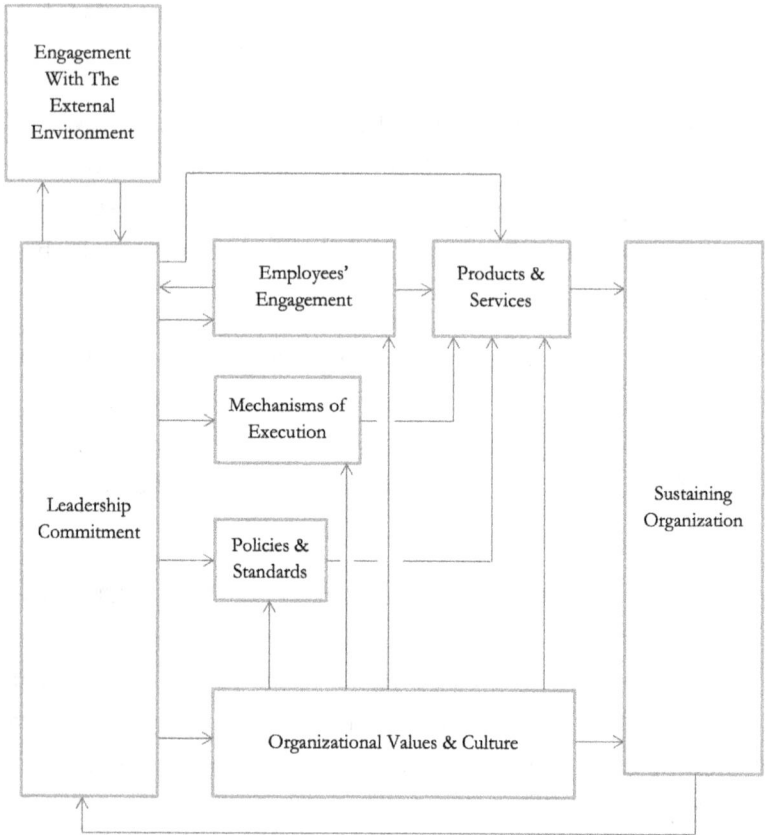

FIGURE 1. Model Representing Characteristics of a Sustaining Organization.

objectives. It can determine supply chain design within the organization, systems, processes (Deutsch & Pécs, 2013), distribution, and extends that effect to the customer. Sustainable supply chain is considered a value-builder for any sustaining organization because the three tenets of sustainably cannot be met or might be difficult to meet without a supply chain that embraces sustainability. Some of the characteristics of a sustainable supply chain (SSC) are as follows:

- SSC integrates all three dimensions of sustainability.

- It is driven by world's sustainability objectives, as well as customer requirements of sustainable products and services such as increasing the life expectancy of products. (Refer to the notes on circular economy in Chapter 1.)

- It contains a monitoring mechanism to ensure suppliers and consumers comply with sustainability objectives, specifically social and environmental sustainability.

- It is based on collaborative relationships with suppliers and customers. Therefore, a sustaining organization involves all stakeholders in their decisions and formulating strategies that require empowering and support.

Continuous Learning

One of the important aspects of any business organization to maintain competitiveness and thrive is the continuity of education and learning of its associates. Organizational sustainability practices, technologies, and strategies continuously evolve which makes it imperative for organizational leaders to seek the flowing of information to their followers. Continuous learning for followers not only addresses their professional and development skills, but also it captures building their intellectual capacities where they can generate new knowledge. Jamali (2006) clarified that effective learning in organization is critical for sustainability performance and innovation. For an organization to become an effective and continuous learner it may need to foster learning in its system as a whole; vision, strategy, structure, culture, processes, procedures, policies, and leadership Jamali (2006). A learning organization may identify needed information, process this information and filter it, and use the outcome to make conscious decisions. Leadership for organizational sustainability can enhance and advance the learning process and contribute vastly to the innovation and sustainability practices within the business facets where followers can engage in solving ethical, social, cultural, economic, and policy problems.

This book adopts what Clifton and Amran (2011) labeled as a transformational approach, which considers the present main economic, social and formal system as the origin and source of unsustainable behaviors and requires a radical transformational change to achieve sustainable world objectives. As a result, leaders need to have sustainable values to create a sustainable world, which can extend to intergenerational periods. Figure 1 illustrates the model presented in this book for the characteristics of a sustaining organization.

CHAPTER 3:
THE INTEGRATIVE APPROACH OF LEADERSHIP

Leadership is not a new term, function, or practice specific to our times, as some scholars portray. On the contrary, many people have practiced leadership for thousands of years. For example, Sennacherib, one of the great kings of Mesopotamia, was a great leader to his people; Alexander the Great was a leader of ancient Greece; Thomas Jefferson, an American founding father and a president of the United States of America; and many more.

Leadership is probably the most misunderstood concept in the social sciences. Leadership should be going beyond the call of duty to achieve group's success through motivating individuals. Many organizations suffer financial, performance, production, and other problems because of poor leadership, while other organizations thrive because of their excellent, energetic, empowering, and supportive leaders. Thus, one might label leadership as one of the most essential ingredients in an organization's competitive advantage. However, many people relate the term *leadership* with hierarchical positions in organizations, others understand leadership as a specific trait, while others understand it as behavior or function. In this book, we refer to the concept of leadership as a function that combines traits and behaviors.

Leadership topics are probably the most researched in academic fields and organizations for more than half a century (Germain, 2012). The confusion in understanding leadership is inherent in the different research schools on the subject and the complexity of human behaviors, motivations, and values. Consequently, many scholars produced different theories, definitions, and styles of leadership, which makes the subject of leadership more complex and more confusing to many practitioners and students. While many different definitions of leadership exist, the common element among the various definitions is that leadership is an influencing process to attain a common goal, as stated by many scholars.

The Integrative Approach of Leadership

The integrative leadership approach includes two or more types of leadership variables and has become common in research in recent years. For example, a leader can use behavior from transformational leadership, such as inspiring followers, with behavior from ethical leadership, such as role-modeling, to achieve specific tasks or influence followers. Because of the fast-changing business environment and the need to develop leaders who can effectively manage their organizations, research on leadership has produced many theories, styles, and leadership concepts. Research on leadership topics and subjects has produced excessive literature, theories, and styles. Therefore, many researchers attempt to use the integrative approach in qualitative and quantitative leadership studies (Lips-Wiersm & Wright, 2012). For example, Anderson and Sun (2017) suggested that transformational and transactional leadership behaviors are not explicitly sufficient to explain leadership behaviors in organizations. Therefore, Anderson and Sun suggested that additions from other leadership styles become necessary, especially in community-oriented and sustainability-oriented organizations that can benefit from servant leadership or ethical leadership.

Some scholars recommended using of integrative theoretical frameworks when studying sustainability (e.g., Amini & Bienstock, 2014; Anderson & Sun, 2017; Lozano et al., 2015). Leadership for sustainability integrates transformational leadership with other leadership theories and styles because sustainability is an interdisciplinary issue and requires leadership theory and behaviors that can address such a complex issue (Burns et al., 2015). Therefore, investigating a leadership style for organizational sustainability requires more than one theory or leadership style. While transformational leadership establishes basic behaviors for sustainability leadership style, this leadership style contains traits and value factors that are significant in this leadership style. As many scholars explain, leaders' values drive their behaviors and enable them to make ethical decisions (i.e., Kooskora, 2013; Marsh, 2013).

The theoretical framework employed in this book is grounded in multiple theories of leadership. These theories include transactional leadership (Bass, 1990), transformational leadership (Bass & Avolio, 1995), ethical leadership (Brown et al., 2005), and servant leadership (Greenleaf & Spears, 2002). These leadership theories are critical to organizational sustainability. While transformational leaders are able to create and manage change needed in achieving organizational sustainability (Burns et al., 2015), transactional leaders focus on performance (McCleskey, 2014) to achieve desired sustainable performance through monitoring of task implementation and continuous development of organizational sustainability strategies (Du et al., 2013). Servant leaders establish the nature of community and world service through sustainability because servant managers are motivated to serve and to meet the interests of others (Stazyk & Davis, 2015). They extend services to society (Liden et al., 2014). Ethical leadership establishes the drivers and motives for leaders to adopt sustainability strategies and go beyond meeting standards and measures since ethical leaders are role models and demonstrate high levels of ethical values. Community-oriented organizations probably need to integrate transformational, transactional, and servant leadership behaviors (Anderson & Sun, 2017). Therefore, the current book employs the integrative approach by integrating four leadership theories (transactional, transformational, ethical, and servant leadership).

Previous research on sustainability mostly used the integrative approach as a theoretical framework. Amini and Bienstock (2014) used an integrative approach to define corporate sustainability and provide a better understanding of this issue. While the proposed framework is integrative, it is not on leadership for corporate sustainability; instead, it is for understanding and evaluating corporate sustainability. Moreover, Burns et al. (2015) stated that an interdisciplinary theory needs to address sustainability issues, and they have suggested that a new understanding of leadership with new skills and values is needed. Burns et al. described sustainability leadership as embedded in three key elements: value-based behaviors, a living process (i.e., awareness, creativity, relationships, and adaptability), and inclusive, collaborative, and reflective. They suggested that leadership for sustainability extends transformational leadership to include change and relations models of leadership. We can conclude that this model of leadership includes classifications of traits and behavioral theories. Additionally, Egbeleke (2014) suggested a management model for sustainability performance management that supports long-term choices based on shared values, the guidance of executions and confirmations, and engagement of all stakeholders to incorporate the triple bottom line for business operations. This model is value-based, an integrative approach to corporate sustainability performance management, and includes classifications of traits and behavioral theories.

Furthermore, Wang et al. (2014) conducted their research based on an integrative approach of leadership theories that included facilitative, collaborative, transformational, full-range, and situational leadership theories, which are variations of the contingency and behavioral theory classifications. Wang et al. considered situational leadership to be results-driven for the benefit of individuals, organizations, or society, while transformational leadership is a change-oriented theory for individuals. The interests that Wang and colleagues addressed were for the common good.

Likewise, Metcalf and Benn (2013) identified leadership styles directly related to organizational sustainability, such as authentic leadership, ethical leadership, and transformational leadership, which belong to the behavioral and trait theory classifications. Additionally, Peterlin (2015) based her study on a framework that integrates leadership with responsibilities to society, empowering followers, bound by context, and leadership skills that can be learned and developed.

It becomes evident that studying or understanding sustainability leadership should integrate several styles i.e., situational, behaviors, and traits. The framework used in this book integrates contingency, behavioral, and trait leadership theories. Additionally, it is evident that the basic attributes of the leadership style for sustainability should: (a) be transformational, (b) be focused on the long-term perspective of the organization, (c) ethical and value-based, (d) build relationships with all stakeholders, (e) be results-driven, and (f) include the common good of the community and followers.

The Employed Integrative Approach of Leadership

As mentioned in Chapter 1, many leaders in organizations remain hesitant to adopt or fail to implement sustainability into their organizations because they do not understand what behaviors they need to master or because they may lack the driving values to do so. Hasan (2018) found that leaders of organizational sustainability might not have established an understanding of their leadership style, specific behaviors, or the combination of behaviors required to achieve organizational sustainability objectives. Leaders of organizational sustainability should know their style, behaviors, and values they should master. Research indicates that one leadership style is not sufficient to achieve required sustainability objectives. Previous researchers and book authors mainly employed or recommended one leadership style, specifically the transformational leadership style for organizational sustainability; others integrated two styles at the maximum.

This book is the first, up to the writing of this chapter, to use such an integrative approach of the employed four leadership styles to find the most dominant behaviors among leaders of organizational sustainability. Since leadership for sustainability is in its initial phases of development, this book illuminates the reader and managers about the justification for using the four styles. Moreover, this book clarifies that the integration of these four styles can provide successful implementation of a leadership style for the success of organizational sustainability adhering to the three tenets of sustainability: social, environmental, and economic. It is vital for any leader to understand the specifics of each leadership style to be able to evaluate his / her style and use a combination of behaviors or one behavior (depending on one's need) to practice.

This chapter illustrates the leadership styles employed in the integrative approach of leading organizational sustainability and the characteristics of each one. As mentioned previously in this chapter, the leadership theories employed in this book are transactional, transformational, servant, and ethical leadership.

Transformational leaders are known specifically for being change-oriented leaders because these leaders transform and change aspects of organizations; therefore, transformational leadership can establish the base of the leadership style to create and manage change needed in achieving organizational sustainability. Transformational leaders might change (a) organizational structure and how teams are grouped or function and (b) organizational culture, product or services, or any other facet of the organization such as: supply chain, bankers, or the relationships with external stakeholders to meet sustainability goals assigned to them. Transformational leaders emphasize the organization and its viability, continuance, and resources.

Transactional leaders focus on transactions with followers to accomplish performance; therefore, they are specifically known as task-oriented. Transactional leaders can achieve desired sustainability performance through three strategies; continuous monitoring of the implementation of sustainability tasks, interfering once the implementation of the sustainability tasks goes wrong, or awarding followers once they successfully implement sustainability tasks. Transactional leaders set performance goals and measures, clarify performance expectations, and create the rewards or the punishment followers will receive. (see Figure 2).

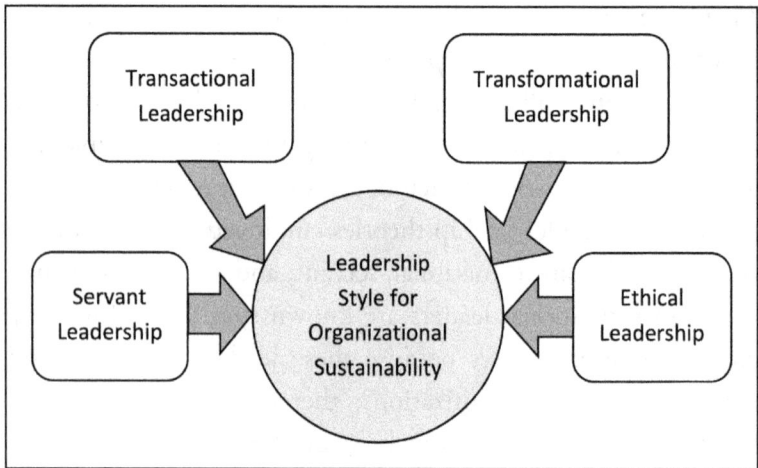

FIGURE 2. The Integrative Approach Employed for Leading Organizational Sustainability.

Servant leaders are known specifically for being relation-oriented leaders, humble, and practicing their functions in altruistic ways. In altruistic ways, servant leaders emphasize their leadership to serve their followers. Therefore, servant leaders establish the nature of both individual and community services that is to serve the interests of the public, and to extend services to the society as pointed by several scholars (i.e., Liden et al., 2014; Stazyk & Davis, 2015); because, they have a higher goal and mission to serve the good of the world.

Ethical leaders emphasize ethics, while integrity is essential in leading organizational sustainability, as suggested by several scholars (i.e., Kim, 2014; Moldogaziev & Silvia, 2015). Therefore, combining the guiding theories overcomes some of the weaknesses of each theory. Figure 2 illustrates the integration of the four leadership theories for organizational sustainability.

This book includes the construct of each leadership style employed to help leaders understand or assess their leadership style. Simply, a leader can ask themselves questions about each one of the elements of the construct to check whether it fits his or her behavioral or personal characteristics.

Why These Theories?

Scholars have different conclusions about the leadership style that is appropriate for organizational sustainability. Some scholars suggested a transformational leadership style (i.e., Senbel, 2015; Tideman et al., 2013). Some other scholars recommended a style characterized by integrity and a long-term perspective of the organization appropriate for organizational sustainability (i.e., McCann & Sweet, 2015; Peterlin et al., 2015). On the other hand, some scholars suggested a strategic leadership style and visionary (Strand, 2014), or altruistic (Peterlin, 2016). Most of the suggested leadership styles for organizational sustainability align with the guiding theories' qualities and behaviors.

The driving factors to use the integrative approach for organizational sustainability can be summarized as:

- Organizational leaders rely on existing leadership styles that cannot achieve organizational sustainability objectives and are not practical for financial management (Leoveanu, 2015; Vinkhuyzen & Karlsson-Vinkhuyzen, 2014). Financial performance measures are indicators of sustainability outcome and sustaining organizational performance (Budiarso & Mir, 2012). Therefore, the mismatch between existing leadership styles and challenges facing leaders continues to occur.

- There is a serious gap in understanding of the appropriate leadership style for achieving organizational sustainability objectives as indicated by many scholars (i.e., Blake, 2016; Elkington & Upward, 2016; Hassan et al., 2014; Hasan, 2018; Kellis & Ran, 2015; Kurucz et al., 2017; Peterlin, 2016; Wang et al., 2014). Therefore, the misconduct of organizational leaders and the failure to achieve sustainability objectives continues.

- A single leadership style is not practical to be the only leadership model for financial management because of many classifications and varying circumstances of these different leadership styles, as suggested by many scholars (i.e., Leoveanu, 2015). It is critical to remember that financial viability of any organization, specifically for-profit organizations, is necessary to contribute towards environmental and social sustainability, as pointed by several scholars (i.e., Perrott, 2015a).

- Without a comprehensive study exploring a new leadership style to achieve organizational sustainability objectives, incapable leaders will continue to rise to levels of power, and sustainability practices will continue to fail, such as financial scandals, economic distress, social injustice (Hasan, 2018; Payne, 2016), and environmental degradation will remain problematic (Virakul, 2016) while financial exploitations in business organizations and governments will continue to occur (Hartman & Ramamoorti, 2016).

In addition to the previous driving factors, leadership for organizational sustainability is still in the introduction phase (Peterlin et al., 2015). It embodies differences from the traditional leadership theories (Shriberg & MacDonald, 2013). Therefore, a critical need exists for additional research and development to secure the development of leadership styles for organizational sustainability, especially a style that emphasizes ethics and integrity. This book provides such research and development.

Construct of Transformational Leadership

Many leaders and readers will ask how do I know whether my leadership style is transformational or another? What are the common characteristics of transformational leaders? This section provides what differentiates transformational leaders from other leaders.

Bass (1985, 1990) advanced the development of the transformational leadership theory. Transformational leaders create a shared vision and mission and build mutual respect and trust with subordinates. Transformational leaders inspire followers to achieve organizational goals by promoting universal values and altruism to the advancement of the group, organization, and society. Bass and Avolio (1995) set forth the behavioral attributes that make up the transformational leader. These characteristics of transformational leaders are idealized influence attributes, idealized influence behaviors, inspirational motivation, intellectual stimulation, and individualized consideration. The following sections explain each one of the behavioral attributes of transformational leadership:

Idealized influence attributes are what others see in the leader, how they perceive the leader's behaviors and values based on his or her influence and interactions with them. Dajani and Mohamad (2016) considered these characteristics as charismatic and emotional aspects of a leader. Since this attribute is *idealized*, leaders reflect their best behaviors and high levels of values to influence their followers. Therefore, transformational leaders act as exemplars and role models for their followers. Consequently, transformational leadership has an ethical dimension embedded within its construct. The ethical dimension of transformational leadership can improve organizational effectiveness, decrease employee turnover, and create an ethical environment where followers resemble leaders' qualities and behaviors.

Inspirational motivation refers to leaders motivating their followers and inspiring them to go beyond their needs and the call of duty. To inspire followers, a leader must be passionate, optimistic, and challenge them. Transformational leaders can inspire their followers by role modeling, communicating effectively with them, and appealing to their emotions, as described by many scholars (i.e., Dajani & Mohamad, 2016; Hemsworth et al., 2013). Role modeling is behaving and reflecting values as a model for others to emulate and act similarly. Followers emulate the behaviors of those whom they admire, like, and are close to them. Leaders should break the barriers between them and their followers through two-way communication and by addressing follower's emotional distress.

Intellectual stimulation refers to a leader's capacity to promote creativity and thinking-ability to become more effective. Leaders can stimulate the brainpower of their followers by allowing them to express their thoughts and exercise their skills without reprisal or fear of making mistakes. Leaders exercising this characteristic of intellectual stimulation can nurture innovation, as suggested by Rowold (2014), by encouraging followers to think creatively, to re-evaluating existing tools, means, and methods, and by endorsing and supporting their ideas to generate new methods to solve old problems rationally (Bass, 1990). Therefore, transformational leaders can encourage and support innovation from their followers.

Individualized consideration refers to a leader's acknowledgment of the individuality and differences each member of his or her team has. Therefore, transformational leaders give significant attention to individuals to develop their skills but do not compare them to others as stated by scholars (i.e., Hamstra et al., 2014). To exercise the individual consideration attribute, leaders should encourage, coach, mentor, and support every team member to reach their potential through supporting their learning new skills, building relationships with them, and caring about them and their ambitions.

The characteristics of transformational leadership can be summarized as:

- They use idealized influence attributes (values and traits) to become role models for their followers.

- They use idealized influence behaviors (actions and decisions) to become role models for their followers.

- They motivate their followers by inspiration and building trust with them.

- They promote the creativity of their followers and support innovation.

- They treat their followers based on their specific differences, build their skills and train them to reach their ultimate potential.

- They change organizational structure, culture, processes and procedures, products or services, or relations.

- They are deontological, which means they focus on methods and means to deliver required performance goals. We will discuss deontological ethics later in this book.

- They are charismatic and emotionally intelligent.

A leader can assess his or her leadership style, whether it is transformational or not, by asking questions on the characteristics of the transformational leadership style. For example, do you consider yourself a change-oriented leader? If so, what types of changes have you made or are making? How do you treat your followers?

Construct of Transactional Leadership

Similarly, the question that arises from managers and readers is about the common characteristics among transactional leaders. Transactional leaders emphasize accomplishing tasks and goals. Therefore, they are efficient and focus on productivity, minimize risks, and are cost-effective. Transactional leaders tend to direct and control the behaviors of their followers to achieve organizational performance goals by maintaining the corporate status quo and reducing concerns, as discussed by many scholars (i.e., McCleskey, 2014). When transactional leaders attain performance goals, they deliver customer satisfaction and efficiency within the organization; however, their relationship with their followers is weak and does not generate loyalty or drive creativity or innovation. Finally, transactional leadership behaviors can lead to high turn-over of employees; because employees are appraised and treated based on their capacity to deliver performance; hence, these leaders leave the organization to other companies who provide a better offer. Transactional leaders tend to have a short-term perspective of their organization by focusing on the organization's financial aspects.

Transactional leadership has three characteristics: contingent reward, active management by exception, and passive management by exception (Dajani & Mohamad, 2016). Contingent reward refers to leader's behavior of rewarding employees upon successful accomplishment of set-forth performance goals. Therefore, transactional leaders encourage competitiveness among employees, and not collaboration. Transactional leaders are driven by their self-interest, and they promote self-interests in their followers; in some cases, they promote unethical behaviors. For example, a transactional leader in an investment or sales company focuses on *meeting the numbers*; therefore, they do not have a shield from committing unethical behaviors. Most of us heard or read about the term *cooking the books*, which refers to falsifying performance results, the financial performance of an organization. Let us not forget the financial scandals early this century that caused many problems, due to which some of us are still suffering.

Active or continuous management by exception refers to the leader's behavior of actively looking for a deviation from standards, policies, and procedures. Once the leader detects deviation, they take corrective action, as pointed by scholars (i.e., Bass, 1990; Dajani & Mohamad, 2016). Continuously monitoring the work and performance of followers reflects adverse values and mindsets such as lack of trust and empowerment. While it might be necessary for specific business environments or industries, employees do not feel comfortable when watched continuously, as if they are doing something wrong.

Passive management by exception, refers to a leader's behavior of intermittently looking for a deviation from standards, policies, and procedures. A leader interferes only when an error or deviation occurs. Passive management by exception, is a behavior of leaders whenever they secure efficient processes and procedures and communicate policies and expectations of performance clearly to followers.

Management by exception relies on the power and authority of the leader; therefore, it can result in unethical behaviors, as discussed previously, when leaders abuse power and authority. Leaders' abuse of power and authority has and can cause corruption, as clarified by scholars (i.e., Bendahan et al., 2015). Consequently, leaders must be aware of the power limits they should exercise so as not to cause harm to individual employees, teams, or the organization.

Power and authority abuse is a toxic leadership behavior in any organization. Not only can the abuse of power and authority cause corruption of leaders, making them exposed and subject to financial exploitations or a prey for other competing companies to reveal trade secrets or manipulate performance, but also, it can result in coercing employees into doing unethical behaviors for the benefit of the organization or the manager, such as sexual favors, covering fallacies of the manager, and manipulating quality of products, to mention a few facts. Moreover, this kind of leader will adversely influence the organization's reputation, potentially causing loss of customers, investors, and talents. In addition, power and authority abuse can promote non-competent individuals to higher levels of employment or management positions; based on favoritism or similar personalities and actions. Moreover, power and authority abusive leaders can cause demoting competent individuals due to rivalry or because individual followers refuse to engage in such manipulative and obscure behaviors.

Transactional leadership can result in unsatisfied employees because of the emphasis on the outcome without regard to the employees, their input, development, or needs. One of the most prized resources to organizations is their employees; therefore, transactional leadership behaviors alone might not be suitable for all situations or all organizations, and for that matter, not for all employees. However, transactional leaders' behaviors of management by exception ensure efficient and compliant employee's behaviors to meet organizational goals and performance requirements. Bass (1985) indicated there is a correlation between organizational effectiveness and transactional leadership in certain situations. However, Bass did not elaborate on what circumstances are suitable to implement transactional leadership.

The characteristics of transactional leadership can be summarized as:

• They use conditional reward (rewarding good performance and punishing poor performance) to manage their followers in meeting performance objectives.

- They continuously monitor work progress and get involved in all stages of production, actively look for deviation from standards, procedures, and policies to manage their followers to meet performance objectives.

- They intermittently look for deviation from standards, policies, and procedures to manage their followers in meeting performance objectives.

- They are efficient in meeting performance goals. They use cost-cutting strategies, product development, and focus on employee productivity.

- They rely on their authority and power to direct and control the behaviors of followers.

- They are task-oriented. Transactional focus on meeting performance goals with little to no regard for employees, their input, ambitions, and / or needs.

- They do not take risks or endorse change or innovation. They maintain the status quo of organizations.

- They seek a short-term perspective for their organization.

- They are utilitarian, which means they focus on end results for the greatest benefit to the maximum number of people.

The transactional leadership style can be used to drive performance and achieve results. Additionally, the transactional leadership style can be used to cut costs, create efficient operations, and increase customer satisfaction. However, any leader practicing this style should be aware of his or her power limits and consequences of solely relying on power and authority since there might be adverse consequences.

Construct of Servant Leadership

Servant leaders are inspired by their intrinsic values and motivation to serve others before their willingness to lead. However, many leaders and readers ask what the common characteristics among servant leaders are.

Servant leaders concern themselves with the common good however, their ultimate goal is to serve their followers' needs. This behavior of servant leaders should be interpreted as leaders doing the work of others or totally ignoring their own ambitions and needs. Servant leadership is about prioritizing the direction of their behaviors. Because servant leaders volunteer to help others meet their goals, they should have professional experience; otherwise, they will not serve. Additionally, servant leaders must be humble and *down to earth* to build quality relationships with subordinates, communicate effectively, and be honest. Whenever leaders provide feedback to their employees, they should be prompt to provide the feedback when needed, not later, honest to tell the truth whether the feedback is positive or negative, and effective to provide guidance.

Servant leaders are humble, altruistic, and act as stewards of others, as clarified by many scholars (i.e., Beck, 2014; Liden et al., 2014). Servant leaders create a trusting, fair, collaborative, and serving culture which can enhance corporate and subordinate's effectiveness. Servant leaders act as stewards and protective of others; however, followers should not misunderstand this behavior, such as refraining from making decisions or facing challenges and complexities when the leader is not present. Followers should not rely on their leaders to protect them from their mistakes. Servant leaders must be aware of this attribute and should empower their followers and build relationships based on trust.

The characteristics of servant leadership style can be summarized as:

- They empower and motivate their followers and nurture innovation to meet performance objectives.

- They act as stewards of their followers.

- They care about their followers.

- They put followers' interests before their interests.

- They are relations-oriented since they build quality relationships with followers based on trust.

- They seek the long-term common good for their organizations, followers, and society.

- They are technically proficient in a particular field.

- They are characterized by integrity and build a culture of collaboration among their followers.

- They are humble and altruistic.

Servant leaders are fulfilled by serving others and doing well to others and the community. The interests of others come before their own interests. Servant leaders' primary desire is to serve as a steward for followers by empowering and motivating them, building a quality relationship, and demonstrating genuine care to followers.

Construct of Ethical Leadership

It is important to know the common characteristics among ethical leaders. Ethical leadership is a broad subject and is closely related and confused with other ethics-based leadership styles such as virtuous, principle-based, covenantal, authentic, and others. Brown et al. (2005) defined *ethical leadership* as the practice of appropriate behaviors through personal actions and interpersonal relationships and the endorsing such behaviors to subordinates through effective communication and decision-making. Ethical leadership reminds us of goodness and sincerity in leaders. Ethical leadership is related to honesty, fairness, trustworthiness, integrity, and caring for others. Ethical values are drivers and enablers of ethical behaviors. Ethical leadership is the integration of ethical values and ethical behaviors as indicated by many scholars (i.e., Brown et al., 20015). Ethical leadership with a high level of values, integrity, and virtuousness can have a high level of immunity against wrong-doing in organizations. Let us remember that situations or contexts can influence leaders to perform unethical behaviors. Therefore, organizations' leaders must pay attention to the organizational environment and evaluate contextual factors to choose the right leader for the specific situation. Ethical leaders are considered role models for their followers, as stated by many scholars (i.e., Brown et al., 2005; Mayer et al., 2009; Stouten et al., 2013).

The characteristics of ethical leadership can be summarized as:

- They are role models for their followers through their actions, decisions, and values.

- They build quality relationships with their followers.

- They establish and enforce the code of ethics within their organizations as the standard of accepted and unaccepted behaviors.

- They are fair, honest, trustworthy, and treat their followers with care.

- They are altruistic, humble, and fair.

- They make decisions for the long-term performance of the organization.

Ethics are an essential element of leadership to avoid confusing tyrants, totalitarians, scammers, manipulators, and terrorists, even though they might have followers and goals. Ethical leadership practices appropriate behaviors through personal actions and interpersonal relationships, and they endorse such behaviors to followers through effective communication and decision-making. It is important to point out that ethical leaders do not practice ethical behaviors only at the workplace, which can be interpreted as masking or proving a case. Ethical leaders practice ethical behaviors everywhere and at all times.

If a leader is not ethical in his or her personal life, then that ingenuity and immoral behaviors will be reflected in work practices one way or another. Examples of unethical behaviors at the workplace are tremendous, including financial fraud, fabricating positive performance results, taking bribes from suppliers, and favoritism. But one of the most destructive consequences of leader's unethical behaviors is creating unethical culture, where followers learn that their leader is not ethical. Therefore, followers replicate their behaviors.

The reader can note that there are commonalities among different leadership styles, which is correct. However, leadership style characteristics are not exclusively specific to a certain style. Servant leaders and ethical leaders are altruistic and humble, which means that servant leaders have an ethical leadership dimension and ethical leaders have a servant leadership dimension. It is vital for organizations to know the characteristics and drivers of leadership styles; because organizations can use them to identify future leaders based on certain needs, select, develop, train, and motivate those leaders. Moreover, organizations can use these characteristics to exclude others from leadership positions. Additionally, organizations should pay attention to situational factors which might drive ethical people to behave unethically. For this book, knowing the characteristics of the leadership styles that are employed in the integrative approach will help organizational leaders understand the appropriate leadership style for organizational sustainability.

A question might arise about how a leader can use these styles in an actual application. Here is an example, suppose that you, as a leader work as a plant manager, where you are responsible for a production line of product A, and 40 employees, where your team produces 100 units per day. And suppose that the organization's vision is to develop its reputation and become the customer's most trusted manufacturer of product A. Since competition in the market is increasing, the chief operating officer (COO) demands from you to put a plan of how to increase market share and to generate more profits. The first action would be to perform market research to find a more efficient production line, i.e., a new technology. You find a modern production line that can produce 100 units per day with 20, instead of 40 employees. Then your plan action strategy is to purchase this production line for its efficiency, saving the salaries of 20 employees (transactional leadership behavior). However, you care about the 20 employees (ethical leadership characteristic) that will become unemployed and have been with the company for many years. Therefore, you become uncomfortable with the letting go of 20 employees and feel their pain in this case, so you decide to do more thinking and try to produce better solutions that adhere to your company's social responsibility, as claimed by its mission and values.

Then, you perform more studies on keeping the entire staff members by purchasing two production lines (change, which is a transformational leadership characteristic), which means producing 200 units of product A every day. But the market share is only 100 units per day. Then, because you as the operations leader have developed quality relationships with the marketing department and the product development department, you ask them to change the packaging size to save money on transportation costs. Moreover, since you have been acting as a steward of your staff and communicating regularly with them on all issues, you get their feedback and thoughts; few of them suggest communicating with the supply chain managers to make the ingredients or parts of the final product of better quality, with less environmental negative effects so that the consumer will see the difference between product A of your company and the competitors' products. This innovation in redesigning the packaging, involving your staff in the process, and including the supply chain managers is a servant leadership characteristic.

The final plan includes two new efficient lines of production, keeping the entire staff, and doubling production and market share with environmentally friendly products. Since the new production lines consume less energy and occupy less space, you can accomplish more savings; therefore, you will be able to add a gym inside the plant for the employees to use, send your staff for additional training and skill development, or increase their salaries. Of course, other scenarios can occur, and rejection from the COO can happen on certain elements of your plan; however, you can always look for ways to optimize social, environmental, and economic sustainability tenets through the use of the four leadership styles employed in this book.

CHAPTER 4:
CHANGE-ORIENTED

Any organization is subject to change. Leaders change organizations, often in production equipment, processes, procedures, culture, materials, products, facilities, teams, organizational structure, strategies, or policies. In many cases, change can be small and not recognizable, yet significant, such as temporarily reassigning one employee to a different function, changing communication methods to facilitate meetings, changing work schedules, or changing process management strategies. Any organizational change should include one or a combination of or all of its composites, structure, processes, policies, products or services, culture, or means. Change in organizations should be expected; as new technologies arise, more efficient processes might be explored, and a different organizational structure might ease the command process and reduce time in achieving objectives. Additionally, new products or services might differentiate one organization from another to keep a competitive edge and adapt to market needs, or cultural change might inspire and motivate other employees to become more productive. For business organizations to survive and thrive, they need to adapt to meet constantly changing business environment demands.

Whether a change in organizations is critical and major or minor and not recognizable, leaders must know the results and challenges which might arise from change. Additionally, leaders must know the process of change and how to manage it. Moreover, leaders should be aware that some changes can cost the organization its existence when not assessed carefully, while other changes might take a few years to show positive results. The success factors for any change can be summarized as:

- Leaders need organizational support to provide the resources necessary to create and implement the change.

- The commitment of top management to empower operational leaders to carry on the change.

- Employees' commitment and participation in the change process.

- Effective communication during all phases of change.

Change happens for one main reason: our interaction with the environment. The environment may be internal or external. Similarly, business organizations interact constantly with the internal environment as well as the external environment. The internal business environment includes employees, peer managers, upper-level managers, and infrastructure and technological resources facilities. The external business environment includes shareholders, suppliers, customers, competitors, financiers, communities, and government entities. However, change has two types: *preemptive* and *responsive*, or as some scholars classified them as *proactive* and *reactive* (i.e., Nadina, 2011). Therefore, change in organizations is an attempt to adapt to business environmental changes.

Preemptive change is a proactive change where leaders actively seek opportunities and analyze the internal and external business environment to better their organization's performance or anticipate a future issue that will hinder their organization's performance. Leaders with vision and long-term perspectives create changes that are preemptive and innovative.

On the other hand, responsive or reactive change leaders do not initiate change. Instead, they wait until failure occurs or when a problem is detected, then leaders respond to adapt to the environmental influencers. Leaders should know that reactive or responsive change can occur while resources are not available or scarce, which strains the organization and might create unsatisfactory or ineffective solutions to the problem detected.

In a proactive change example, Hasan and Roach (2010) explained that when they were working on one of the engineering projects, the applicable energy standard during the design did not require an *economizer*, which is an energy-saving mechanism used in the heating, ventilation, and air conditioning (HVAC) systems, because of the location of that specific project. However, the design team pursued an analysis of energy savings and financial costs for this mechanism. When the analysis indicated the advantages of this mechanism, the design team decided to implement it on the project. The estimated energy savings were $15,223 per year, and the simple payback was 4.1 years, which was a great decision. That meant the financial cost of the mechanism used would be paid in 4.1 years, while the client would save $15,223 per year afterward.

Therefore, as an operations manager, you can find ways and methods to anticipate the road ahead and explore options and solutions to contribute to achieve sustainability objectives. You do not have to wait for a problem to occur or pressure from business environmental conditions to direct you for specific strategies and procedures. One method is to go beyond the standard requirements and improve the quality of products and services beyond accepted levels, maintaining changes' financial viability.

Change-Oriented Leaders

One of the characteristics required in leaders for organizational sustainability is to be change-oriented leaders. What is meant by change-oriented leaders? This term means that leaders should be open to change, and they should have the mindset for change. Therefore, leaders should not be caught up in the status-quo of the organization to eliminate risks associated with changes and reject change or discourage it.

Change is the main character of transformational leaders, as mentioned in Chapter 3. Transformational leaders create substantial change; however, transactional leadership can have a critical effect on the change required for sustainability because transactional leaders use rewards to encourage sustainability implementation, as suggested by Blake (2016). In addition, transactional leaders create incremental changes, maintain corporate status quo, and reduce concerns or risks (Dajani & Mohamad, 2016; McCleskey, 2014; İşcan et al., 2014). Additionally, servant leaders can be of critical effect on change implementation because they can enhance the effectiveness of managing change, as suggested by Bin Ibrahim and Bin Don (2014). Therefore, a change-oriented leader can be transformational, transactional, or servant and can apply either style in different phases or types of change towards sustainability. Additionally, leaders can create substantial changes or minor and incremental changes or changes towards sustainability or play a supporting role to enhance the effectiveness of managing change.

Upper-level leaders are expected to make substantial changes since they have the power and authority to make strategic and transformational changes. Operational managers are expected to make incremental changes within their functional boundaries or support and enhance the effectiveness of managing change, i.e., operational leaders can use transactional and servant leadership behaviors for change towards sustainability. Hasan (2018) found that most sustainability leaders (93%) are considered change-oriented leaders, whether they initiated and implemented incremental, transformational, or facilitated change. Most sustainability leaders (79%) use transactional leadership change themes (Hasan, 2018). However, different companies use different approaches to change.

There are a few reasons that cause operational leaders to make incremental changes towards sustainability which can be summarized as:

- The organization's upper-level managers have already developed all organization's facets (structure, culture, policies, and processes . . . etc.) to embrace and implement sustainability strategies; therefore, operational leaders have minimal chances to make transformational changes.

- A leader must go through the bureaucratic culture or the increased hierarchy levels within the organization to get a decision or strategy approved or even discussed. The bureaucratic process hinders and discourages leaders from initiating changes, therefore, they become comfortable and adapt to making changes within their functional areas. Transactional leaders support bureaucratic culture and systems, as described by Ogbonna and Harris (2016). Upper-level leaders can additionally be transactional, where they must monitor, check, and approve everything in a way that does not empower operational leaders to make transformational changes.

- Operational leaders might be afraid of failure or rejection; therefore, they tend not to create risks or substantial changes that can fail, leading to demotion or even discontinuing employment.

- Operational leaders often demonstrate commitment and adherence to policies and procedures to demonstrate loyalty to the organization, which is often appreciated by upper management.

- Operational leaders often prefer to witness quick performance results of changes and initiatives they make and promote. Therefore, the changes they make are incremental and minor and primarily based on the positive financial outcome.

Operational leaders need to understand that sustainability changes should not always be based on the financial outcome or approved in advance by organizational policies. Operational leaders can work with upper-level managers to change policies and sell their ideas and strategies to them to contribute to the social and environmental dimensions of sustainability while maintaining positive financial outcomes. Therefore, operational leaders must change their mindset and become change-oriented leaders.

Change-oriented behaviors are consistent with existing literature on leadership for organizational sustainability since they are change-oriented, as supported by many scholars (i.e., Burns et al., 2015; Klingenberg & Kochanowski, 2015; Metcalf & Benn, 2013; Tideman et al., 2013; Wang et al., 2014).

The strategies of changes that operational leaders can use in accomplishing sustainability tasks can be summarized as:

- Tie changes to measures and policies; consequently, leaders use checklists to clearly track tasks and communicate vision, goals, and expectations.

- Tie changes to operational efficiency such as operation costs, financial efficiency, and minimizing risks. Therefore, leaders frequently check progress and monitor goal accomplishment, and similarly, they tie employee's rewards to performance while holding others accountable for their failures when needed. Operational efficiency changes can include consolidating project tracking tools to save time and effort, reducing staff, cost savings, using technology to facilitate communication and reporting. However, leaders should be aware of the social dimension of sustainability when approaching operational efficiency changes.

- Maintain procedural and distributive justice during change since followers might develop feelings of insecurity, lower commitment, and lower productivity during change. Deschamps et al. (2016) clarified that effective leaders demonstrate commitment to organizational justice during change.

- Tie changes to employee development and rewards when change is initiated by upper management, i.e., facilitate managing change, such as providing training and support to subordinates to facilitate implementing change initiated by upper management. Facilitating the implementation of changes and providing support to followers align with servant leadership behaviors in supporting change management as supported by many scholars (i.e., Bin Ibrahim & Bin Don, 2014).

These strategies, methods, and means are consistent with existing literature on transactional and servant leadership behaviors. Transactional leaders are efficient leaders and are known for increasing productivity, reducing production and operational costs, and for enhanced customer service and quality (i.e., Kumar, 2014; Sadeghi & Pihie, 2012; Zdanyte & Neverauskas, 2014). Transactional leaders focus on goals and performance and they monitor work progress continuously or periodically, while they reward employees based on a good performance. Moreover, as supported by many scholars (i.e., McCleskey, 2014), transactional leaders minimize risks and use rewards for performance.

Business Process Reengineering

The previous section explained minor or incremental changes that do not shake or alert upper management of risks or financial loss or expenditure. This section includes explanations of transformational changes within business operations and required or initiated by operational leaders. The business process achieves predetermined business goals through sequential activities. For example, the process of producing canned vegetables includes several steps and activities in sequence before one can hold a canned vegetable in his or her hands.

On the other hand, reengineering or redesigning a business process is a full-scale or whole system change to the process objectives and the activities or steps sequenced to achieve objectives. Business process reengineering or BPR is a management strategy that was significantly developed by Crosby, Ishikawa, Deming, and Juran in the 1970s (as cited in Chountalas & Lagodimos, 2019), and it can result in structural changes within the organization; however, the focus of this section is on the business process transformation.

The purpose of redesigning a process is to become more effective, more efficient, improve customer service, and improve quality. However, in a sustaining organization, BPR can result in environmental or social changes or both, within the business unit lead by an operational leader. For the purpose of this book, effectiveness means doing the right thing, and efficiency means doing things right. Business process management has been studied by scholars, where many well-defined methodologies broke throughout their research. For example, Total Quality Management (TQM), Six Sigma, Lean production processes, and other methodologies are a few approaches that are centered on process reengineering, quality management, and process effectiveness. This science of process engineering or process management is vital as it determines the total performance of any business organization.

Business organizations face many challenges in what we witness as an ever-changing global economy. For them to survive and thrive, they need to constantly keep a competitive edge to outperform their rivals in one way or another. This cannot be done with a rigid and bureaucratic system. In a traditional organization, process reengineering starts from the top, a top-down approach. However, a sustaining organization should start from the bottom, so it is a bottom-up approach. Operational leaders are close to production and services processes, therefore, they become more knowledgeable about their operations, and they know first-hand what should change and when change is needed. The BPR in a sustaining organization should have the following specifics:

- BPR is a bottom-up approach.

- BPR can include social and environmental changes.

While there is no agreed-upon methodology of BPR, it requires upper management support, followers support, open culture that accepts and encourages transformational change, flexible thinking, and effective communication. The business reengineering process has a significant impact on the success and efficiency as well as effectiveness of organizational performance when used correctly and when top management supports the initiative, and when employees are involved in the process supplied with sufficient resources. Another success factor to the business reengineering process is the effective communication channels within the organization.

Change Process in Organizations - Recommendation

As mentioned above, change happens due to our interactions with the environment, internal or external, business environment. A leader in a sustaining organization should always be analyzing the business environment to check for effectiveness, efficiency, technological updates, alignment, performance measures, and innovations. A change in organization can be within its structure, culture, policies, facilities, or strategies, which we can call *organizational* change. Other changes can be in organizational production equipment, processes and procedures, materials, or products, which we can call, *process* change. Once a leader analyses the business environment, they should identify a need for change.

Let's assume there is a need in team structure, where a need exists to change teaming from functional teams to matrix teams. Once a leader identifies the change needed, they should identify the new setting, who will be the team leader, who will be on each team, etc. The new team structure will require leaders to align with the overall organizational structure and chain of command. Once leaders align the new change with organizational structure or process, they should evaluate the risks associated with this new change. If the new change fails, the matrix team structure in our example; leaders should reevaluate this change in relevance to the business environment. Once the change passes risk assessment, leaders should test the new change. In our example, the matrix team structure should be tested in real life work tasks and their performance should be evaluated. If the new team fails in performing their tasks with respect to expected results, then leaders should reevaluate the functions given to the team, team capabilities and skills, and their knowledge. Team leaders might need training in management or communication, some team members might need less responsibility, or some members need more challenging assignments. Once the team passes the testing phase, leaders should implement the new teaming structure throughout the organization. After a certain period of implementation of the new change; leaders should evaluate the performance and its influence on the organization. If it fails, then leaders should evaluate what went wrong and how they can fix it. Once the change implementation passes the evaluation, leaders should sustain it. Please refer to Figure 3 on the following page for the organizational change process diagram.

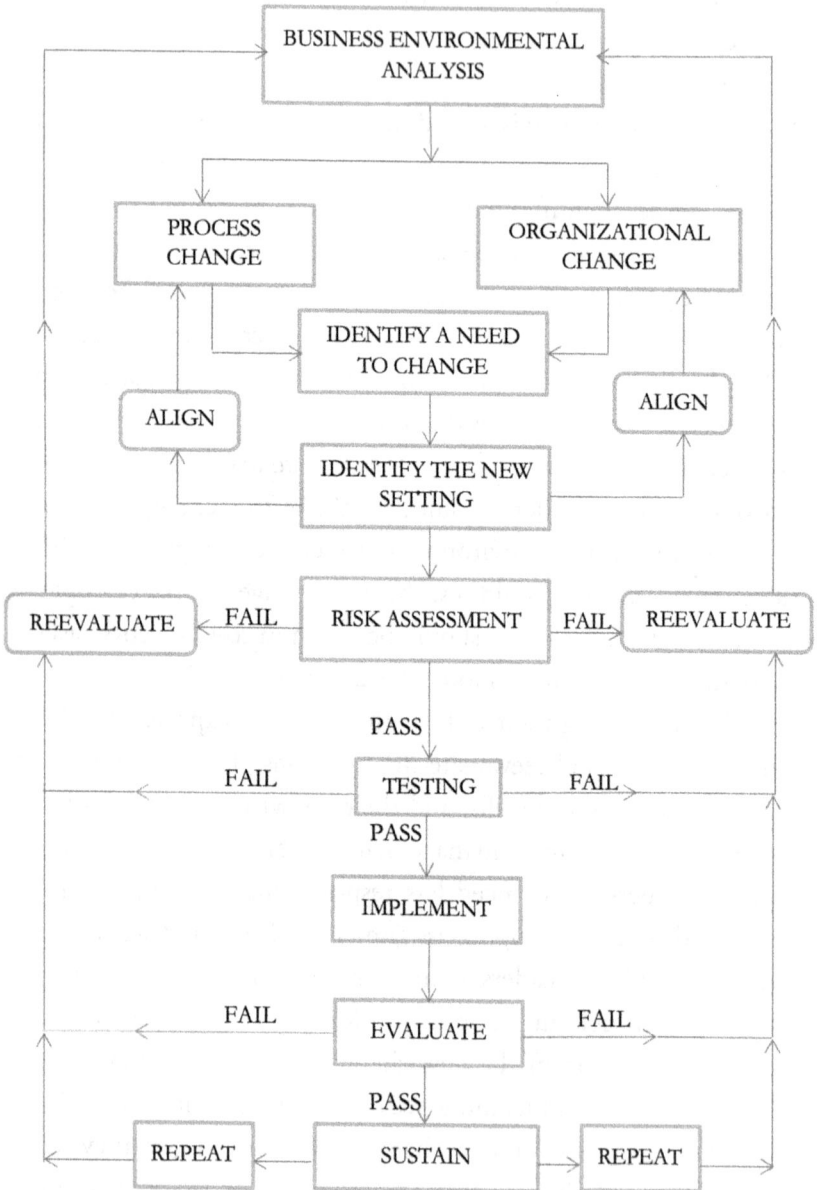

Figure 3. Organizational Change Process Diagram.

Change Resistance

In the past few decades, many organizational leaders faced many challenges, including globalization, technology, increased competition, environmental, and social. Organizations that do not change to adapt with these challenges will either perish or experience extreme losses. While many operational leaders initiate or support changes within their organizations, not all changes are successful. The biggest challenge to change is change resistance. Change resistance can be from other managers, upper management, and from subordinates. Management-level change resistance can be because of threats to their position of authority, increased responsibilities that might come with change, and even the possibility of eliminating their positions or downgrading them. Additional change-resistance factors at the management level can be because change might be challenging to their skills or because they might lose control over resources. For example, restructuring an organization to become flat might mean eliminating front line management positions or increasing staff for middle managers. In contrast, subordinates' resistance to change can be because of the fear of change as it brings uncertainty. In inspiring research, it has been reported that 70% of change initiatives fail (Burnes & Jackson, 2011). Organizational leaders should understand the consequences of resisting change, specifically when that resistance originates from subordinates and continues after change implementation. Resting change can create divergent behaviors, which are negative forces impeding the success of change and are different from the norms and commonly accepted behaviors of a social unit as defined by scholars (i.e., Agboola & Salawu, 2011). Divergent behaviors resulting from resisting change has been documented by scholars (i.e., Agboola & Salawu, 2011), categorized as:

- Production divergence is any behavior that negatively influences productivity, such as intentionally working slowly, producing lower quality products and services, taking unnecessary sick leave or absence from work, and working fewer hours, or even conducting personal business while on an organization's time.

- Property divergence is any behavior that affects the production facilities, equipment, and infrastructures such as stealing from the organization, sabotaging of equipment or properties, intentional waste of material, using organization's transportations for personal usage, and giving away products to others.

- Social divergence is any behavior that negatively influences the social fabric and justice norms within the organization such as gossiping, favoritism, and building coalitions against leaders and manipulating others.

- Interpersonal divergence is any behavior that can take the form of physical violence, verbal abuse, and sexual harassment.

- Representation divergence is any behavior that negatively represents one's own organization such as talking negatively about the organization in conferences among peers or revealing organizational trade secrets to competitors.

Leading change for organizational sustainability is an essential skill to be added to modern leaders as the business environment is constantly changing and because sustainability is a complex challenge. Leaders should understand the barriers of change needed towards sustainability and should anticipate resistance resulting from these barriers. However, proactive leaders can ease the change process if they communicate effectively with their employees and motivate and support them morally and emotionally. Additionally, change agents should be aware of their own actions and competence as it might be a possible barrier to change, reflecting the poor quality relationship with employees.

CHAPTER 5:
RELATION-ORIENTED AND COLLABORATIVE BEHAVIOR

Leadership for organizational sustainability reflects on the interactions and relationships a leader builds and maintains with stakeholders, followers, and peers. Through relationships, leaders fulfill their goals in serving the common good and their organizations. The need for relations-oriented leaders for organizational sustainability becomes critical because as the globalization and complexity of the business environment grows, the political systems become complicated, and technology advances exponentially. Therefore, leaders should master effective communication, become collaborative leaders, and build and sustain relationships through their functions. As indicated by several scholars, leadership is a social phenomenon. It occurs in social group settings such as schools, business organizations, churches, government agencies, sports teams, political parties, and more. Relationships and alliances can be strengthened throughout leaders' interactions with others, and solutions to complex problems such as sustainability may become possible.

One of the characteristics required in leaders for organizational sustainability is to be relations-oriented, collaborative, and inspiring, which is consistent with research on leadership for organizational sustainability. Leaders for organizational sustainability should be excellent in communication and focus on the relationships with all stakeholders (i.e., Herremans et al., 2016; Kurucz et al., 2017; Senbel, 2015), inspiring and emotionally intelligent (Senbel, 2015), and collaborative (i.e., Burns et al., 2015; Galuppo et al., 2014; Peterlin, 2016). The requirement of being a relation-oriented leader for organizational sustainability has been mentioned in many studies (i.e., Burns et al., 2015; Kurucz et al., 2017; Senbel, 2015).

Chapter 3 explained the leadership styles used in the employed integrative approach for this book, and it is clear that transactional leaders direct and control followers' behaviors by exchange of rewards and penalties as indicated by some scholars (i.e., McCleskey, 2014). Therefore, the relations they build are based on interests, not shared values. On the other hand, transformational leaders engage followers in decision-making, as explained in a study by Ölcer et al. (2014). Additionally, transformational leaders treat followers as valued ends, not means, recognize their contributions, build their confidence, and support them in their roles as claimed by many scholars (i.e., Carter & Baghurst, 2014). Moreover, transformational leaders mentor followers, as McCleskey (2014) indicated. However, servant leaders are relations-oriented leaders, since they care about their followers, the environment, and the world (Peterlin, 2016), empower and motivate followers (Greenleaf & Spears, 2002; Liden et al., 2014), build trust, communicate effectively, and provide honest feedback (Beck,

2014), and they are stewards of others (Peterlin et al., 2015). Servant leaders might even sacrifice their interests for the sake of their followers' interests.

Furthermore, ethical leaders are relations-oriented leaders since they build quality relationships with their followers, are role models, and build trust and values through their relationships with others. Characteristics and links between ethical leadership and relationship with followers that is based on dignity, support, and fairness are clear in the works of many scholars (i.e., Asif et al., 2020; Brown et al., 2005; Ko et al., 2018; Mayer et al., 2009; Stouten et al., 2013). Hence, the relations-oriented characteristic is not absolutely exclusively relevant to a specific style. Throughout this chapter, the focus is on building relations, effective communication, and collaboration of leaders.

Change Process in Organizations – Recommendation

As mentioned previously, change happens due to our interactions with the internal or external business environment. Therefore, a sustaining organizational leader should always analyze the business environment to check for effectiveness, efficiency, technological updates, alignment, performance measures, and innovations. A change in an organization can be within its structure, culture, policies, facilities, or strategies, which we can call organizational change. Other changes can be organizational production equipment, processes, procedures, materials, or products, which we can call process change. Once a leader analyses the business environment, they should identify a need for change. For example, assume there is a need in team structure, where a need exists to change teaming from functional teams to matrix teams. Once a leader identifies the change needed, they should identify the new setting, who will be the team leader, who will be on each team, etc. The new team structure will require leaders to align with the overall organizational structure and chain of command. Once leaders align the new change with the organizational structure or process, they should evaluate the risks associated with this new change. If the new change fails, such as the matrix team structure in our example, leaders should reevaluate this change in relevance to the business environment. Once the change passes risk assessment, leaders should test the new change.

In our example, the matrix team structure should be tested in real-life work tasks, and their performance should be evaluated. If the new team fails to perform their tasks with respect to expected results, leaders should reevaluate the functions given to the team, team capabilities and skills, and their knowledge. Team leaders might need training in management or communication, some team members might need less responsibility, or some members need more challenging assignments. Once the team passes the testing phase, leaders should implement the new teaming structure throughout the organization. After a certain period of implementing the new change, leaders should evaluate the performance and its influence on the organization. If it fails, then leaders should evaluate what went wrong and how they can fix it. Once the change implementation passes the evaluation, leaders should sustain it. Please refer to Figure 3 for the Organizational Change Process diagram.

Leader's Relations

Relationships within the function of leadership are complex and must be addressed by leaders to become successful in achieving organizational sustainability objectives. Herremans et al. (2016) discussed three different types of relationships a leader can have with different stakeholders: (a) power-based or one-sided relationships, (b) conflicting relationships, and (c) collaborative relationships. However, only two types of relationships are discussed in this book since conflict can arise from power-based relationships and practices. Therefore, organizational sustainability leaders can face two types of relationships as follows:

- Leaders can face relationships that impose decisions and actions on the leader to comply with and execute. These types of relations can be in the form of direct response to upper management requests in the organization or to respond to stakeholders' interests. Additionally, authoritative relationships can exist between an operational leader and their followers whenever their behaviors and performance are related to punishment and rewards. This relationship type is also known as a self-interest relationship. Followers will only cooperate and execute sustainability directives when they realize they will be punished if they do not do so and rewarded when they successfully do. Therefore, this type of relationships is based on power, where whomever or whichever party possesses more considerable power dominates the relationship over the operational leader.

- Leaders can face relationships where operations leaders collaborate with stakeholders, peers, and followers. Because adherence to sustainability objectives is voluntary, operations leaders should support and increase the contributions of others; throughout their relations, towards achieving organizational sustainability objectives. Leaders should build those collaborative relationships on their commitment to the cause they support, fairness to everyone involved, and respect. Treating followers with respect and fairness strengthens their organizational citizenship, a key ingredient in achieving organizational sustainability objectives. Therefore, operational leaders should demonstrate these behaviors and build trust with all involved parties in their function as sustainability leaders.

Executing promises, treating followers as valued ends, supporting them in their roles, building their confidence, recognizing their contributions, and involving them in the decision-making process are significant factors in building trust and strengthening follower organizational citizenship. Additionally, operational leaders can use several strategies to build trust with followers, peers, and other stakeholders. For example, leaders should know how others perceive them; then they should do something different to correct the wrong perception. Leaders can also provide promises they can keep while they celebrate milestones along the way. Moreover, leaders must understand that their speeches cannot change the wrong perception if followers do not trust them. Trust is the crucial factor in building confidence in leaders.

Hasan (2018) found that sustainability leaders treated their followers differently and used different leadership styles to establish those relationships. For example, 57% of participants described servant leadership relationship themes, 36% described transformational leadership relationship themes, and only 7% described transactional leadership relationship themes. Participants in Hasan's study described in their answers that the following relationships leaders have with their followers within the themes of a servant and transformational. These relationships were stewardship, supportive, motivating creativity, respect, humbleness, tolerance, care, shared approach, and empowering individualized consideration. One can notice clearly that transactional leadership treatment of followers is not standard among sustainability leaders since it is based on formal relationships, which means the leader treats his / her followers as a *boss*, and at the same time, followers are considered means in the process of organizational performance.

Organizational Citizenship

Organizational citizenship behaviors (OCB) are essential to both individuals and organizations. OCBs have been identified by many scholars as the voluntary behaviors that are advantageous to the organization while not part of the reward or recognition system (i.e., Ölcer et al., 2014). Employees might engage in such behaviors when they identify themselves with the organization, be motivated, and possibly be committed to their organization. OCBs are considered essential for higher organizational performance and leadership effectiveness. The benefits of followers' organizational citizenship are:

• Organizational citizenship increases followers' engagement in their organizations. Employee engagement is the passion, commitment, and voluntary contributions of employees to the success of their work and organization (Carter & Baghurst, 2014).

- Organizational citizenship increases followers' morality, becoming like guardians of organizational assets, reputation, and objectives. In addition, because followers identify themselves with the organization, they commit to the organizational culture and moral behaviors required to increase performance.

- Organizational citizenship lessens followers' behaviors that conflict with organizational benefits, such as sabotage, stealing, working fewer hours, and much more.

Identification with the organization refers to harmony and belonging to an organization one demonstrates (Deichmann & Stam, 2015). Followers consider leaders to be role models therefore, their contributions and initiatives to benefit the organization increase when they see that their leader demonstrate organizational citizenship behaviors. A leader's role is vital in the performance of organizations. Effective leaders for organizational sustainability inspire followers and create passion in them towards achieving envisioned goals.

Specific Relationships with Followers

Organizational sustainability leaders can use entirely or partially the following specific behaviors to establish their relationship with their followers towards achieving organizational sustainability objectives:

- Leaders should treat their followers as their team captains and work side-by-side with them, provide guidance to everyone on the team, and be hands-on leaders and do whatever their team members are doing.

- Leaders should become approachable to their team members, have an open door policy where followers feel comfortable coming to the leader with concerns and use a coaching approach. Leaders who distance themselves from their team members might not build collaborative, trust, and respect-based relationships.

- Leaders should not micromanage their followers, provide them the resources and tools they need, provide followers with autonomy to make their decisions, support them, appreciate them, and let them do what they do best.

- Leaders should treat their followers with fairness, transparency, dignity, care, respect, and be accountability. It is better for the leaders and the organization and followers when followers work with you rather than for you. Therefore, leaders should consider their followers as their coworkers and not subordinates.

- Leaders should be emotionally intelligent and accommodate emotional issues or followers may suffer.

- Leaders should communicate with their followers frequently and interact with them one-on-one. Through open communication, leaders can understand their followers and know them. However, leaders should right-size their communication, keep them together as a team, and work with them individually on their specific function because every follower is different and has a different skill set.

Leaders for organizational sustainability using relation-oriented strategy should not mean that they should not use transactional or formal relationships with their followers. In some cases, formal relationships should be the case. Such cases are when followers prefer a reward and punishment system or require a directing approach in their functions. Usually, followers require a directing and control approach to their behaviors when they are in the early stage of their careers.

Communication

The concept of effective communication was clarified by Djordjevic and Cotton (2011) as two-way communication, which entails the receiver sending a message back to the sender indicating an understanding of the original sender's message. Therefore, communication is a process through which sustainability leaders and followers can establish an understanding of shared values and common goals. Many scholars claim that effective listening is a significant factor in effective communication, but also it is a part of two-way communication. Effective listening is not hearing other's voices or reading their messages; it is an active and thoughtful receiving of messages and deciphering them to understand them. Effective listening requires leaders to fully be engaged in the process of communication and not merely pretend to do so. Suppose a follower is speaking to you at your office and your side shoulder or back is turned to them, or you are typing on the keyboard, or even looking at your cellular phone. In that case, which is not effective listening, this behavior breaks the communication system, and sends many wrong messages to your follower. If, after receiving the message, you still do not understand it fully, ask questions to get more information or clarification. Organizational sustainability leaders should be aware of the following aspect of the communication system when communicating sustainability messages to their followers:

- Leaders should ensure that the sustainability message is clear, meaningful, and understandable by recipients because sustainability is a complex and challenging issue. Recipients understand the message from their viewpoint. Therefore, leaders should be aware of the level of knowledge and skills followers have.

- Leaders should ensure that communication channels are effective. The medium through which leaders send their messages must be reliable, credible, and trusted.

- Leaders should ensure that the recipients understand the message as they intend it, which means leaders should allow for feedback about their message from followers. This part makes up the two-way communication functions.

- Leaders should ensure they communicate with their followers in a timely manner.

- Leaders should ensure they get feedback from recipients that the message have been delivered and understood.

The above elements of the communications system can be of strength and barriers to communication. The most critical element in the communication system of sustainability messages is the understanding of shared values. What then are the shared values of sustainability? Shared values in business organizations are the social conditions, environmental flourishing, and economic growth outcome of the business. Therefore, shared values refer to the business model and its policies, strategies, operations, and decisions that produce this kind of outcome. Social conditions refer to followers' work-related conditions as well as their well-being and life in general, and the social conditions of the community. There-fore, organizational sustainability leaders should ensure that any business-related message reflects shared values, as well as be clear and understandable.

Collaborative Leaders

Leaders for organizational sustainability make decisions that are long-term, and intergenerational. Since sustainability is a value-based strategy, decision-making in sustaining organizations or for sustainability should be a value-based decision. Value-based decisions formulate the roots for successful organizational sustainability. Organizational leaders should justify their decisions towards sustainability because that will influence others' adoption and compliance with such decisions. Value-based decisions for sustainability in organizations are supported by many studies (i.e., Ljungholm, 2016). Meaningful advancement toward sustainability requires leaders to collaborate with stakeholders in the long-term and strategic decision-making (Ljungholm, 2016). Collaboration and partnership with external and internal stakeholders for successful organizational sustainability is supported by many scholars (i.e., Klingenberg & Kochanowski, 2015, Kurucz et al., 2017; Perrott, 2015a; Zdanyte & Neverauskas, 2014). Leaders for organizational sustainability should adopt strategic and long-term decision-making as indicated in many studies (i.e., Doorasamy & Baldavaloo, 2016; McCann & Sweet, 2014; Perrott, 2015b; Peterlin et al., 2015; Strand, 2014; Williams & Trunbull, 2015). Therefore, organizational sustainability leaders should make strategic decisions and be collaborative.

In making strategic decisions for organizational sustainability, leaders can benefit from the following recommendations:

- Sustainability leaders should make shared and strategic decisions by gathering related facts from different sources and stakeholders, including followers. The next step is to then look at different options to get consensus on one option to make a long-term decision based on the best possible option and continuously evaluate results.

- Sustainability leaders do not need to get 100% of the required information to make decisions. Hasan (2018) found that several sustainability leaders gather between 75% and 80% of the information they need to make decisions.

- To make a successful, shared, and strategic decision for organizational sustainability, sustainability leaders, can either get consensus from all participants on a decision or gather information from all stakeholders and decide based on the common opinion.

- While most leaders use transformational and servant leadership decision-making themes for organizational sustainability, some leaders use transactional leadership behavior. Hasan (2018) found that 64% of sustainability leaders use transformational and servant leadership decision-making themes. However, the transactional leadership decision-making theme can be related to fewer years of experience in sustainability leadership. According to Hasan, the average number of years of practice of participants in managing others for sustainability tasks and who described using the autocratic decision-making theme (transactional leadership) was 8.4 years, 9.8 years for the participative decision-making theme (transformational leadership), and 18.5 years for participants who described using shared and strategic decision-making (servant leadership) behaviors. Beck (2014) indicated that the more time one holds a leadership role, the more they demonstrate servant leadership behavior. Therefore, leaders might transition from transactional decision-making to transformational and later to servant leadership decision-making themes as they spend more time in leading others for organizational sustainability.

Organizational sustainability leaders collaborate with external stakeholders as well. Organizations operate within communities that they influence and use resources from, whether these resources are human, natural or both. Therefore, sustainability leaders collaborate with community leaders, interest group leaders, local government officials, and others who can take responsibility in making decisions towards sustainability practices for the organization. Collaborative leaders do not make sustainability decisions alone; rather, they allow all involved parties to participate in addressing the challenges facing them (Ferdig, 2007). It can be said that the complexity and severity of the environmental, social, and economic problems humans face cannot be solved or addressed by a single party, by business organizations, by government agencies, or by special interest groups. Therefore, it becomes evident that collaboration for formulating and executing organizational sustainability strategies require the collaboration of all stakeholders, and it is the responsibility of the sustainability leader to bring those stakeholders together to make such decisions.

CHAPTER 6:
CREATES AND SUPPORTS SUSTAINABILITY-ORIENTED CULTURE

Scholars and practitioners refer to organizational culture as the shared beliefs and values and the norms practiced by individuals and groups within an organization, which shape their behaviors. In other words, good organizational culture is considered the main driver for performance and for the promotion system. Consequently, employees' behavioral response to a change in the business environment is an indication of cultural strength or weakness. Organizational culture is the secret ingredient that glues teams together towards achieving their goals. It is the recipe by which individuals assemble into teams and teams into groups, forming one organization performing at much more of their mathematical sum. Organizational culture is the way to create winning organizations that survive challenges and difficult times. A strong culture creates loyalty and belongingness for individual employees. On the other hand, harmful or toxic cultures can destroy organizations. Organizational culture differentiates one organization from another since it represents how things are done within a specific organization and defines its relationships with internal and external stakeholders and expectations.

Organizational development is concerned with how business facets (a) are aligned and used to maximize organizational output and performance; (b) adapt to the environment; and (c) survive their rivals. An effective organization achieves its goals by aligning strategy and culture with structure and products or services. Organizations cannot attain their goals without stewardship and leadership. Organizational structure is the chain of commands and the communication standards throughout the organization. Organizational structure and culture form the mechanism through which strategies and decisions are executed and missions are supported. It is essential to differentiate between organizational design and organizational structure. Organizational design is the framework that organizational structure builds on. Some organizations fail to integrate culture and design when structuring or restructuring an organization as they might focus on either one. To clarify, organizational structure is the hierarchy of the organization describing the responsibilities, roles, and expectations from employees at each level within the hierarchy and the authority channels. Organizational design is the identity of the organization that defines leadership, vision, mission, culture, values, and relationships with stakeholders, and production flow. Therefore, organizational design includes structure and culture, and it is a system to execute organizational strategies.

Focusing on the design part of the organization is a shallow process, as it does not integrate management changes, procedures, team-building, or processes. In addition, focusing on the organization's structural developmental element creates a temporary effect or outcome, it is not supported in the core of the organizational design. While each process, development and design, and culture and structure, are positive and necessary to the organization, however, when misaligned, this can create ineffective organization. Bate et al. (2000) introduced a culturally sensitive restructuring model for organizational development and design. It starts with the culture to set up the grounds for structure, while leadership is a process institutionalized across the organization and not restricted to top management.

Types of Organizational Culture

The most critical aspect of globalization for an organization is the cultural differences across nations and the differences in laws and policies. For example, all businesses shut down during prayer times in Saudi Arabia. Therefore, any company operating in that country should understand cultural differences while leadership should compensate for potential lost productivity. Research indicates there are four main organizational cultural types; however, in this book, I label them in a shorter, yet comprehensive way, following studies that documented types of organizational culture such as Ogbonna and Harris (2016) and Maharani and Roshandi (2019):

- *Market culture or competitive culture*: This type of organizational culture has little regard for employees since the organization adopting this culture focuses on performance, getting results, and generating profits. Therefore, this culture promotes competition among employees, less collaboration, and business politics. Employees working in this type of culture strive to enhance their skills and performance to get promoted. Moreover, this culture causes employee burnout and a higher turnover rate. In market culture, profit comes first. Because this type of culture is market-driven and based on competition the focus of leaders is on external stakeholder relationships.

- *Change culture or innovative culture (adhocracy).* This type of organizational culture is characterized by change, innovation, and leadership support. Employees are encouraged to challenge existing methods and standards, while leaders are risk-takers. In this culture, change and innovation come first. The change or innovative culture may exist in high-tech, industrial, manufacturing, and start-up organizations.

- *Bureaucratic culture or clan culture*: This type of organizational culture can be found in family businesses or similar organizations that are run as a clan where it is characterized by members with strong bonds, working longer hours than typical business, as everyone holds the back of each other, and have higher goals than the paycheck. Clan culture is additionally characterized by productivity, flexibility, executing orders, and providing employees with opportunities to express their voice and ideas. In a clan culture, people come first, therefore, the focus is on teamwork, and achieving organizational goals.

- *Community culture or hierarchy culture*: This type of organizational culture can be found in government and healthcare organizations, and it is characterized by following procedures and processes that have been established for a long time. Leaders monitor adherence to policies and procedures. Leaders tend not to change things or take risks because they try to keep costs minimum and fear failure. Procedures, policies, processes, and guidelines come first in a hierarchy culture. This type of culture typically is established from long-term, while decision-making follows structured hierarchy.

Bureaucratic and community cultures might be found in non-profit organizations, while innovative, change and competitive cultures might be more suitable for higher performance requirements in private and for-profit organizations. While these are separate and distinct types of organizational cultures, there is no reason for leaders not to blend different types to become more competitive, generate more profits, and contribute to organizational sustainability. Organizational culture remains an overlooked subject yet critical for the survival and performance of any organization. As a leader, can you determine the type of culture within your organization? Do you think it is the proper culture for increased or higher performance? Do you think it is the proper culture to help you succeed in your role as a sustainability leader?

Strong organizational culture is a requirement for organizational effectiveness and success. Higher performance is achieved through strong culture because of the following reasons:

• Strong organizational culture is a competitive advantage for the organization. Leaders can get more work accomplished when organizational culture builds on hard work, collaboration, and teamwork, for example.

• Through a strong organizational culture, information and knowledge can be shared quickly, which shortens the learning curve for new hires and creates a learning organization.

Followers share resources, help one another, provide guidance to each other, and accomplish tasks as a team, where everyone gets credit for work.

- Through a strong organizational culture, leaders can facilitate and implement change easily since they can predict what is accepted and what is rejected by their followers.

The following elements characterize a strong organizational culture:

- Homogeneous responses and behaviors across the group of followers towards a particular event or issue, as clarified by Bushardt et al. (2011). When followers behave similarly, and their opinion or views of an issue are the same, that means the culture is strong because they all have shared values and beliefs.

- The culture has a significant influence on followers' behaviors. In some cases, leaders do not need to rely on authority to emphasize or demote something; they instead defer to the culture they have supported.

- Attracts top performers and retains top performers even in challenging times. A strong organizational culture can substitute or complement the reward system of pay, promotions, and bonuses. It is easy to get rid of low performers; however, it is challenging to keep top performers. Leaders must be aware of culture as an enabling organizational facet to reward employees by being flexible, respectful, and empowering.

- A strong culture is also reflected in the interactions of followers. Followers talk to one another; they share information and discuss good and bad elements of the organization with no fear of retaliation from leadership. Every member of the organization, regardless of their subculture, has a voice and is acknowledged for their contributions, i.e., a culture of inclusiveness.

Weak organizational culture does not attract top performers; it generates financial losses, bad reputation, weakens future growth, and can negatively affect the organization's survival. Leaders must understand their organizational culture and try to change a weak culture if it exists, to a strong culture. For managing change, please refer to Chapter 4 of this book.

Cultural and Global Influence

Globalization, advancements in technologies and political system reformations have made it possible for organizations to operate across their country's borders. However, this trend in organizational internationalization creates many challenges to the leadership and adds to the complexity of operations. Legal implications, ethical standards, technological complications and security, organizational structure, social and cultural facets of the organization are all parts of these challenges.

Any organization is assessed by its success. The success of an organization depends on managing its dimensions. Hult et al. (2007) identified five of these dimensions; strategy, leadership, culture, structure, and the processes. When an organization expands its operations across the borders, its capabilities and mindset in the mother country operations or headquarter will not work anymore as the environment of business changes. However, the leadership of that organization has the power and holds the keys to decision-making to allocate resources, change the structure, and adapt culture to the new environment. Globalization is an organizational strategy that leaders consider carefully and recognize its challenges. Leaders should plan to instill worldwide culture and to align global structures and processes to meet organizational objectives.

Organizational effectiveness relates mission to strategy. McCann (2004) indicated that organizational effectiveness measures how successful an organization achieves its mission through strategies. The changing environments of businesses, especially in the global environment, create complexity and demand new skills, knowledge base, and capabilities. Hault et al. (2007) found that organizational structure follows strategy as leadership, strategy, and culture drives structure and processes. Moreover, they found it particularly important for a global organization to build a global corporate culture to support structure and processes to drive organizational performance. The capabilities of organizations mean the capabilities of individuals, teams, and the organization as a whole to align with each other to meet environmental changes and challenges. This alignment requires that leaders of organizations be flexible and adaptable.

The global environment requires leaders to seek alliance, partnership, or joint ventures to create a global and larger scale of operations across countries or regions. The underlying driver will always remain in the organizational culture shaped by the leadership and their vision, innovation, and open thinking. However, organizations' leaders must balance their openness and their capabilities in managing interdependencies, risks, and costs created in the process, with their ability to adapt. For example, mergers or alliances can cease organizations from existing if not managed well. Larco (2009) believed in the hybridization of the global and the local cultures and aspirations in globally lead organizations or projects. Hybridization of local and global cultures can reduce fear from globalization, minimize resistance from the local markets, and create a bank of resources to support either market.

Organizational Culture and Organizational Sustainability

Many organizations have created new strategies and developed policies and processes to adhere to sustainability initiatives; however, many other organizations need to change in their leadership style and cultural values. Organizational sustainability requires leaders to create strategies for implementation and change or emphasize the culture within the organization (Elkington & Upward, 2016), since sustainability is concerned with fairness, justice, and care for the community and the environment, as clarified by Stuart (2013). Effective leadership and organizational culture are key drivers of effective decision-making for sustainability (Perrott, 2015b). Creating a culture of shared sustainability values that extend beyond the organization's boundaries and includes stakeholders, governments, suppliers, and customers can lead to innovations for organizational sustainability and may create a competitive advantage for the organization. In a seminal article, Ehrenfeld (2005) emphasized the role of cultural values in organizations as the fundamental element in creating sustainability. For its importance, some scholars considered culture in sustainability to be the fourth pillar of sustainability, as Laine (2016) mentioned.

Many corporations and government agencies incorporated social and environmental strategies in their business operations. This integration can be seen as a reflection of their culture. At the inception of any corporation, leaders shape and frame organizational culture. New leaders arise within that culture, but later the new leaders might take actions or initiatives to change organizational culture based on their vision, beliefs, and business-environmental changes. Upper management or the board of directors can embed sustainability into the organizational culture by making sustainability part of organizational norms and values.

Additionally, operations leaders can provide training to their followers on sustainability issues and increase their skills and knowledge, engaging customers and other stakeholders in the process. Leaders should note that changing or copying organizational culture is extremely difficult if not impossible, because a rich organizational culture is shaped over many years. Therefore, it cannot be copied if a manager or a leader leaves for a different organization and tries to replicate the previous organizational culture.

Sustainability culture in any organization is reflected in its employees' behaviors, interactions, and daily life in that organization. For example, in late 2018, I was called by a recruiter from a leading manufacturing company that specialized in producing a sustainable product worldwide. By talking with the recruiter, I found out that their employees work 10 to 12-hour days and more in the department that I was recruited to work with. Yet, the founder of that company enjoys a lavish lifestyle. Therefore, if I had joined that company, I would have been expected to work long hours daily and almost cut my family time to zero. While that company was producing a sustainable product, it had little regard for its employees' needs. Therefore, I did not see myself fitting into that culture.

Leadership and Culture

Leadership and culture have an interplay where one influences the other. For example, in the past century, it was accepted to smoke inside workspaces; however, it is considered taboo or even illegal to do so. Workspace layout has changed as well, where cubicles and open office layout dominate the current space design instead of offices. In addition, many organizations adopt telework policies, where employees can work from home. Let us not forget the role of technological advances in changing organizational culture. It will not only be unaccepted, but also strange if an engineer asks for a T-square and an inclined drafting desk for their office since software advances made it possible to design a building totally using a computer. It is the responsibility of leaders to design a culture that can facilitate change towards sustainability. In addition, one cannot lead others without understanding and adhering to their values and beliefs, which are the ingredients of culture. Additionally, members of any organization formulate expectations and principles of behaviors from their shared values and beliefs. Organizational leadership should be collaborative, with the ability to influence others, and share decision-making to build a sustainability culture and sustainability mandates, as Perrott (2015b) clarified. Hasan (2018) found that the cultural elements which leaders promote to support sustainability fall into two categories:

- Leaders promote elements that strengthen followers' culture: such as increasing followers' confidence, encouraging their creativity, empowering followers, promoting teamwork, promoting organizational success, and promoting virtue ethics.

- Leaders promote elements that strengthen leader's culture: be a participative leader, promoting sustainability efforts and issues in personal and business life, and collaborate with stakeholders. Additionally, leaders perform to be supportive, altruistic, collaborative, to promote change, value followers and their input, and to use effective communication.

An organizational culture that supports sustainability should be built on trust and transparency, caring for employees and the world, empowering employees to think creatively, and allowing them to pick their tools and means, and to make their own decisions. Sustainability supports a culture that encourages innovation and risk-taking and forgives followers' mistakes. Additionally, the culture should increase the confidence of employees and their awareness of values and goals as well as of sustainability issues. Moreover, leaders should support a culture of training and educating their followers.

Characteristics of Sustainability-Oriented Culture

Sustainability must be part of any business unit within an organization that desires to become sustaining. Most readers understand that top leaders and executives establish organizational culture, but we must realize that operational leaders can also support or create their own business unit's culture. Sustainability, as stated previously in this book, should be the DNA of organizations, i.e., in their culture as well as business. The following cultural characteristics can shape sustainability-oriented culture:

- *Honoring the psychological contract.* Most researchers tend to agree that the psychological contract is the mutual unwritten rules and expectations between the employer and the employee. Researchers such as Romanelli (2018) and Caldwell and Hasan (2016) emphasized that these psychological contracts are rarely perceived but are critical to organizations' success and creating high performance. Psychological expectations can develop and change over time as leaders build their relationships with their followers and employee's position changes. For example, followers can expect longevity of employment, rewards for hard work, respect, voice, promotions, fair treatment, safe environment, bonuses, etc. Similarly, organizations can expect loyalty, hard work, contributions beyond the call of duty, working overtime when needed to finish a project, protecting the organization's assets, etc. One way to honor the psychological contract is to have leaders treat their followers as valued ends and partners. Psychological contracts can have an endless list, but most important is understanding that followers are humans and go through problems in their personal lives. Therefore, leaders must find ways to deal with the emotional distress followers can go through. Another essential element of psychological contacts is for leaders to provide training for their followers and to develop their skills.

  By honoring the psychological contract, leaders can harvest the benefits of mutual trust that builds on values and moral duties owed to followers, between followers and the organization. First, however, leaders must manage followers' expectations because followers might have more expectations than the organization can or will provide. Similarly, leaders can have expectations from followers that they may not be aware. Therefore, managing the psychological contract relies on managing the relationships with followers and is based on effective communication. Failing to honor and manage the psychological contract can result in loss of productivity, diminished loyalty and trust, and higher employee turnover rates.

It should be mentioned that the psychological contract does not only exist between organizations and employees, but additionally, it exists among employees themselves. Therefore, leaders are responsible for fostering teamwork spirit and collaboration among followers.

- *Fostering an ethical culture*, Romanelli (2018) emphasized that building relationships between leaders and followers should be the leader's priority at the beginning of employment and should stress moral values and sustainability within the organization. Operations leaders should introduce followers to the organization's ethical code of conduct, provide training on ethical principles, and act as ethical role models. Ethics should be instilled within the culture and not be the responsibility of the human resources management (HRM) department; it must be the responsibility of everyone within the organization. To achieve, leaders must institutionalize ethics into the daily life of the business (Weber, 1993). Therefore, ethics should not merely of memorize the principles in the codebook; they should be an instinct of followers in their daily business life. Organizational ethical culture can be reflected in their decision-making process, policies, and reward system by promoting those who demonstrate commitment to moral values and integrity.

- *Creating change-ready culture.* Leaders have to address their continuous and diversified needs. Organizations' extinction is often the result of failure to prepare and address emerging needs for new products and new markets, i.e., the customer of tomorrow (Dervitsiotis & Kanji, 1998). While any change might involve a change in culture and people, leaders should foster diversification or rotation in positions where followers can perform several tasks and functions and learn different skills for the organization's future. Innovation requires followers to be involved in the decision-making process and for the organization to have open communication. In addition to these steps, leaders must engage followers in the process of change and appreciate and respect their participation.

- *Discouraging consumerism culture.* The United States of America is the most consumption nation in the world. Each person in the USA has twice as much the ecological footprint as in Europe (Brown & Vergragt, 2015). One might question this cultural element, as it is related to increased profitability. How can we reduce consumerism and keep profitability simultaneously? What is meant by consumerism is the excess of consumption beyond satisfying needs. For example, one person living in a single-family house does not need two television sets; one is sufficient. Generating profitability can be achieved by increasing the market share of products and services with higher quality and better services. Additionally, profitability can be achieved by efficiencies in material usage and recourses exploitations. Brown and Vergragt (2015) mentioned three mechanisms that might create a transition beyond mass consumption: social movements, government policies and laws and creating new business models. However, a radical change in culture might be needed to create a different lifestyle focused on human welfare. Leaders can choose to transition the culture within their organizations by following a bottom-up approach instead of a top-down approach, where they encourage and support ideas and suggestions from followers to reduce consumerism within the organization and in their lives.

Culture of consumerism is the most dangerous threat to sustainability on Earth (Wilk, 2017). Currently, 20% of the world's population is consuming more than 80% of the available resources, while responsible for a similar proportion of environmental pollution, i.e., 80%. (Wilk, 2017). Imagine if we provide the other 80% of the world's population with the same comfort and convenience as the 20%; what will happen to the ecological system? On the other hand, injustice will continue to exist if we keep the status quo; suffering elevated temperatures, warfare, poverty, and diseases. Therefore, reducing and discouraging the culture of consumerism on the one hand and solving the product issue from its roots on the other hand, might be the solution for consumerism culture.

During the writings of this chapter, a friend of mine who lives in Germany told me that the university town of the city of Tübingen will start charging waste taxes starting on January 2021, on plastic disposables such as silverware provided with meals at fast-food restaurants to cover the costs of removal of these items from trash cans. While this step might be helpful in reducing the culture of consumerism, it might be better if fast-food meals come with no plastic silverware at all. Consumers should have their own metal silverware in their cars and clean them after usage. In some cases, a radical transition in cultures might be the best approach. Leaders for organizational sustainability should be aware of the importance of the cultural element and use towards achieving organizational sustainability objectives.

- *The culture of inclusion and diversity.* Organizational culture should be diversified and inclusive. Diversification includes generational and gender differences and sub-cultural differences. A sustaining organization should be a representation and a reflection of the bigger society in which it exists. Inclusion means creating a business environment where all workforce regardless of their diversity grouping, feel belonging to the organization and are encouraged to reach their peak performance and position. Inclusion is to treat followers as valued ends and tap into their creativity and talents. There is an increase in the diversified workforce in organizations as the border barriers are broken by technology, and the global market is open for competition. For example, it is not uncommon to find a Korean male or female software engineer flying to California working under the leadership of a French manager in a company owned by a Chinese or Indian national. Neera et al. (2010) indicated that managing diversity is crucial to reaching the top in the new millennium. Leaders and managers of organizations should acknowledge that diversity impacts organizational culture and leadership. This acknowledgment should act as the direction to create or modify policies, procedures and recruitments. Some scholars indicated that women are more transformational leaders than men, then recruitment and promotion policies might need to be altered to allow more women to become leaders for more effectiveness.

There are many other things leaders can do to foster and lead diversity in the workplace including training programs, providing equal opportunities to everyone, encouraging tolerance, and discouraging discrimination. Diversity will remain the highlight of the workplace in the new millennium, and organizations must adapt to this fact and must know how to manage it to stay competitive. Globalization and demographic differences are critical elements for leaders so they can understand how to influence and lead followers with different values, beliefs, cultures, expectations, backgrounds, and genders.

- *The culture of engagement.* Leaders for organizational sustainability should not treat their followers as passive recipients of orders, policies, and procedures. Leaders should strive to engage their followers in the process and get their feedback. The creation of a feedback system fosters a culture of engagement and creates greater ownership and participation of followers, such as in schools (Hatchimonji et al., 2018). The surprising fact is that research reports close to 67% of employees consider themselves not engaged in their organizations as documented by Smith et al., (2016). Organizations with engaged employees are more profitable, provide better customer service, and are more innovative than other organizations, as Smith et al. reported. Engaged employees demonstrate commitment to their organizations and work, demonstrate higher performance levels, and become a source of competitive advantage for the organization. Leaders for organizational sustainability should foster high trust culture and respect for their followers to engage them.

Sustainability leaders have attributes of trust, empowerment, altruism, foresight, internal motivation, communication, and service, and they create a value-based culture that can enhance corporate and follower's effectiveness. Therefore, sustainability leaders must exemplify appropriate commitment behaviors to a financial exploitation-resistant culture (Hartman & Ramamoorti, 2016), environmental protection and development, and social justice. A culture of organizational sustainability is a vital path towards achieving organizational sustainability objectives and requires changes throughout organizational facets, from upper leadership to front-line leaders to relationships with employees, suppliers, and community, as clarified by scholars such as Stillman (2016). Change towards sustainability starts with a vision for sustainability from upper leaders, followed by execution from middle and front line leaders. Moreover, organizational sustainability leadership should be collaborative, positively influencing others, and sharing decision-making to build sustainability culture and execute sustainability mandates (Perrott, 2015b).

The application of leadership behaviors in creating or promoting a culture for organizational sustainability indicates that leaders should create or promote a value-based culture aligned with universal values (Burns et al., 2015; Peterlin et al., 2015; Williams & Trubull, 2015). Specifically, it should be based on integrity as supported by the research of Puni and Bosco (2016) and shared sustainability values that extend beyond the company's boundaries to include all stakeholders, government, suppliers, and customers, as indicated by Perrott (2015b). In doing so, leaders should utilize a combination of sustainability culture, servant leadership, ethical leadership, and transformational leadership behaviors. Furthermore, the culture should be built on trust and transparency, caring for employees and the world, allowing and empowering employees to think creatively, pick their tools and means, and make their own decisions, but forgive their mistakes. Additionally, a culture for organizational sustainability should increase employees' confidence and awareness of values and goals. Moreover, leaders should support a culture of training and educating their followers. Organizational leadership has a primary responsibility of creating sustainability-oriented culture.

CHAPTER 7:

EFFICIENT, MOTIVATIONAL, AND ENDORSES INNOVATION

As mentioned in previous chapters, natural resources are limited, and the financial viability of organizations is necessary for their survival and critical for sustainability. Therefore, leaders for organizational sustainability should be efficient. Organizational sustainability is a multidimensional phenomenon that integrates sustainability concepts and quality improvement characteristics (Schalock et al., 2016). Schalock et al. (2016) conceptualized organizational sustainability as having a continuous accepted outcome, maintaining stable operations with human and financial resources, creating knowledge, enhancing the capacities of human resources, and maintaining an effective and efficient value-based organization. Schalock et al. (2016) viewed quality improvement as a continuous process that integrates organization's self-assessment, preparation, application, and evaluation. Without a viable and acceptable financial outcome, an organization might not meet its obligations or contributions to sustainability or its survival. Thus, it is a fundamental and critical requirement of organizational leaders to exercise efficient operations and management to generate profit, and they must be efficient with products and resources. Efficiency can be a determinant factor in hiring a leader since organizations seek leaders who can identify and develop the skills of their followers to meet required performance objectives.

Efficient Leaders

Organizational sustainability maintains proper organizational operations of efficiency and effectiveness combined with continuous quality improvements and building high-performing teams, emphasizing transactional and transformational leadership with strategic implementation skills. Organizational effectiveness measures intended results from both customer and organization's views, while organizations' efficiency is a measure of intended results viewed from internal financial and process perspectives (Schalock et al., 2016). Schalock et al. (2016) conceptualized leadership for organizational sustainability as transformational with strategic execution skills and efficiency in operating the organization.

Leaders of organizational sustainability can enhance employees' knowledge, skills, and competencies to benefit organizational effectiveness, increase production or operation efficiency, work, and product quality, which can be leveraged to become a competitive advantage for the organization. Therefore, sustainability is not only greening things, such as recycling and using energy-efficiency strategies, but also using proper financial practices and making sure the decisions that leaders make today have a positive impact on their organizations in the future. Sustainability leaders should focus in their operations on cost efficiency, increasing productivity, minimizing risks, and monitor work progress frequently. Transactional leaders are known for increasing productivity, reducing production and operational costs, and for enhanced customer service and quality, as indicated by several scholars such as Sadeghi and Pihie (2012), Kumar (2014), and Zdanyte and Neverauskas (2014). There are several business elements where leaders can demonstrate their skills in efficiency management such as facility operations and maintenance, product design, production lines, transportations, and distribution. However, other business strategies leaders can exhibit efficiency, but may pose social concerns. These business facets are the automation of jobs and cutting jobs.

Automation and Artificial Intelligence

The development of new technologies can lead to the replacement of employees with machines. It is no longer an imagination of a science fiction writer that machines can take over tasks that humans traditionally performed. It is a scientific fact that much more artificial intelligence (AI), and robotics development are forthcoming to markets and businesses. One of the significant employment industries that will be negatively influenced by the development of AI and usage is the transportation industry since the software is being developed and tested to replace drivers. As documented by the Bureau of Labor Statistics (2020), 47% of U.S. jobs are at high risk due to automation in the next 20 years ("Assessing the Impact," 2020).

Moreover, beyond software and robotics, AI continues to

advance at exponential rates that target highly skilled employees. To have a clear picture of how businesses and employees can be displaced by software or other forms of technology, think about how much business traditional rental cars lost because of the creation of Uber and other platforms and how automation displaced labor in manufacturing and farming industries. Other jobs that will have technologies, AI, and automation that will replace human labor are customer service, cashiers, inventory recording and product stocking, local clothes and shoe retailers, and even professional jobs.

There are small gadgets in the market that can be connected to your car's computer and performs a diagnosis of the vehicle to send you a message to your smartphone of any problem found in your vehicle. While this device saves car owners thousands of dollars, it takes away business from mechanics. Imagine that in the future, engineers and scientists invent a specific machine that can measure your temperature, blood pressure and even is capable of analyzing your blood automatically by a small blood drop that can be withdrawn through a needle. This process can then scan your body or the place of pain in your body, ask you specific questions on the screen, and print out a medical report and a prescription for your medication in a few minutes. That can replace doctors or much of their function, which is an extremely critical and important career in human life and history.

It should be noted that human-integrated machines, robots, or chip-connected humans, are beyond the purpose of this book since these issues are concerning ,serious, and complex, which pose more ethical issues and influence the future existence of the human being race. One of the most precious human heritages inherited throughout thousands of generations is hand-writing.

Because of software and computers' inventions, hand-writing as a skill and human-cultural element is vanishing, and now is being replaced by voice typing software. Fast-forward 100 years from now; will the human race keep the hand-writing skill? What will happen then if energy-dependent technologies quit operating?

Some researchers claim that advances in AI and automation in general will create new opportunities and create new economies relying on previous advances in several industries such as the software industry. Simply put, machines need labor to create, operate, and maintain them. Moreover, machinery and automation increase productivity; therefore, they increase revenues and profits, which can be used to expand businesses or increase labor salaries. Sustainability leaders should not understand from the previous discussion on automation that the intention is against industrial development. The alarming issue is the rate at which AI and automation continues to advance, which is higher than the rate at which industries can re-skill or prepare their employees for the new technology. In addition, many of the technological advances and automation continue to replace human labor, specifically low-paying and routine jobs.

Sustainability leaders must be cognizant of the effects of adopting automated processes that displace labor. Moreover, sustainability leaders should be transparent with their followers on future planning and offer training and re-skilling. Additionally, sustainability leaders must reduce the adverse effects of automation and AI, generate benefits, and solve problems for all involved parties. Moreover, sustainability leaders shall evaluate any economic decision based on its effects on all parties involved for the long-term and not the short-term.

Cutting Jobs or Salaries

Another strategy leaders tend to use, specifically when they hold a new position in management, is to cut jobs or salaries to save money and generate efficiencies. One form of cutting jobs is what we witnessed in the past century and continues to occur: offshoring or outsourcing jobs to foreign countries. Outsourcing jobs to countries where labor and production costs are fractions of their cost at the mother country resulted in lower product prices, more profits to organizations, and created job opportunities and developed economies in the host countries. However, the effect caused vast unemployment in mother countries of the outsourcing organizations, which increased economic pressure on individual laborers and governments. Cutting jobs or salaries and the do-more-with-less mentality might be the standard operation for some organizations to cut costs and become more competitive. However, empathetic leaders are less likely to do so, even if they are directed by upper management even in weak economic environments, as found in Dietz and Kleinlogel's (2014) study. Therefore, sustainability leaders should be empathetic and not focus on their team due to efficiency requirements. However, to become aware of organizational requirements, they should balance their people-orientation characteristic with their task-oriented one.

Many scholars agree that sustainability leaders should be efficient, task-oriented, and generate profits (Perrott, 2015a; Schalock et al., 2016; Tideman et al., 2013) and practice efficient management (Kumar, 2014; Neverauskas, 2014). However, many leaders might fail if they focus only on efficiency by cutting jobs or salaries or adopting automated processes that displace employees because these acts negatively influence the organization. For example, cutting jobs will lead to employee burnout, degrading performance, and lessening organizational citizenship. Similarly, cutting salaries will result in job dissatisfaction and hinder employee engagement and contributions, resulting in employee turnover. Additionally, adopting automation that displaces employees has negative social impacts. Not only should leaders focus on social and environmental sustainability, but also leaders should consider organizational efficiency and financial viability of their organizations as a necessary facet to enable contributions towards environmental and social sustainability (Perrott, 2015a). Therefore, sustainability leaders should choose effectiveness over efficiency and balance over having a single-sided focus. However, sustainability leaders should maintain and seek efficiency in all business areas where, and when possible, reasonable and sustaining.

Motivational Leaders

Recent economic challenges and increased market competition have clarified and emphasized the importance of the role of individual employees in service and production. Recognizing this fact makes leaders explore strategies to make their followers more effective, motivated, committed, and more competitive. Motivating followers is one of the most challenging tasks of leaders. Many factors can affect follower motivation, such as the relationship between leaders and follower, the values embraced by the followers, the emotional status of the followers. Other factors that affect follower motivation include the leader's behaviors and values and how they act as a role model, and the support or reward type the follower gets from his or her leader.

Researchers documented that achieving organizational objectives and goals is rooted in motivating employees. Leader's values are critical in influencing employees' perception and commitment towards social initiatives. Transformational and transactional leaders influence the development and motivation of followers and influence the organizational goals achievement and the individual follower's goal achievements. Motivating employees depends on the relationship between leaders and employees, which is driven by the values and behaviors of leaders. Motivation can be linked to situations as well. Motivated employees demonstrate commitment and loyalty to their organizations, and they work on attaining better capabilities as they realize their value to the organization.

Moreover, their performance might be higher than non-motivated employees. According to Zareen et al. (2015), motivated employees can become a competitive advantage for the organization. Employees' knowledge, skills, and competencies can benefit organizational effectiveness, increase production or operation efficiency, work, and product quality, and be leveraged to become competitive. Similar to motivated employees, committed employees value their association with their organization. They are loyal to their organization. Thus, they are less likely to leave the organization and demonstrate support to their organization in achieving goals and initiatives. In addition, they pursue higher performance for their tasks and organization. Therefore, committed employees can be considered a competitive advantage of an organization.

We know that not all people or followers can be motivated using the same behaviors, incentives, or strategies. Followers can have two different motivational values; one type is considered pro-sustainability values while the other is not pro-sustainability values as claimed by research conducted by Ribeiro et al. (2016). Individuals with dominant intrinsic values such as freedom, justice, or valuing nature, are pro-sustainability and social justice, while individuals with dominant extrinsic values, such as power or public image, are less concerned with human rights, welfare, and the environment. Therefore, sustainability leaders must know the motivational values of their followers. Ribeiro et al. (2016) concluded that value-based sustainability performance assessment of universities could support and increase awareness towards sustainability development. Consequently, ethical leaders with deeply rooted values can promote and achieve organizational sustainability, raise awareness of values that are the basis for needed change towards sustainability, and embed sustainability values into organizational performance assessment. Hasan (2018) found that 71% of participants use transformational leadership elements to motivate their followers. For example, they used inspirational motivation, individualized consideration, and idealized influence. Some other leaders, 14%, use transactional leadership strategies to motivate followers using monetary awards (Hasan, 2018), or commending their performance among team members to shine their image. Furthermore, about 14% of leaders use servant leadership strategies to motivate their followers (Hasan, 2018), such as effective communication, training, and supporting followers in their tasks. Therefore, we can conclude from Hasan's research that 85% of followers have pro-sustainability values since they are motivated by elevating their values and awareness to sustainability through effective communication and support.

Motivating followers is a challenge to leaders and organizations. The question that remains is how to motivate followers? To answer this question, we should know what motivation means and entails. The *Dictionary of Business and Management* (2006) defined motivation as creation of stimulation, working environment, or incentives that empower other people to perform at their best to achieve organizational objectives. The *New Penguin Business Dictionary* (2003) defines motivations as the effort and drive to satisfy an individual need. For example, a person might work, and work harder because of a need for money and status. From the previous definitions, it is apparent that motivation results in behavior to satisfy a need or needs. Motivation can be external, such as creating a satisfying environment, a stimulating job, incentives, or internal to satisfy follower needs, such as earning a desirable salary or buying a house or a new car. For this reason, motivation has been of high interest to managers and organizations, as it is the driver for higher productivity and job satisfaction. Abraham Maslow introduced the concept of the hierarchy of needs theory in 1943 which focused on the human needs that energize, dictate, and maintain behavior (as cited in Huitt, 2007). Maslow (1943) divided human needs into two categories, deficiency needs and growth needs. Each lower need must be met within the deficiency needs before moving to the next higher level (Huitt, 2007). Maslow's growth ultimate needs are for one to become transcendent in their environment, which is to be become wise and help others fulfill their needs.

The following strategies can be used to motivate followers to attain sustainability objectives:

- *Creating a satisfying job.* The priority for an employee is his or her family, but also, work to get personal satisfaction, a stimulating work, and find meaning for their life through jobs. Naturally, it becomes evident that the first most crucial factor in affecting a stimulating job is work-life balance. If an employee is stressed because of family issues, they won't be productive or satisfied as they should be. In the same manner, if an employee is stressed from their job, that can be reflected on their lifestyle and family members outside working hours.

Work-life balance is achieved by follower's ability to balance personal life needs with job needs. Working longer hours and or on weekends can shift the balance of this equation. A motivational leader should know how to provide that balance for his or her followers. Kanwar et al. (2009) clarified the negative consequences of the conflict between family and work. Therefore, many organizations realized the importance of this factor and provide programs that help their employees manage the balance between personal life and work. Among many other things, the organization can adopt some of the following recommendations: provide flexible work schedules, teleworking, onsite childcare, fitness center facilities, alternate work schedules, and employee consulting programs.

- *Providing a secure job.* In the past few years, we noted an increasing number of employee layoffs, organizational restructuring, downsizing, and mergers which have led to less employee loyalty. As a result, job security is an essential factor in motivating followers. Employees seeking employment need to make sure that an organization will not let go of them after a few months. Lorincová et al. (2019) found that more than 87% of study participants rated job security as a motivational factor in achieving sustainability objectives as important to particularly important. The feeling of having a secure job can be considered a motivational factor for followers to increase their productivity, efficiency, and loyalty.

- *Providing inspirational motivation and intellectual stimulation.* A charismatic leader knows how to engage his or her team in their work. Moreover, that directly affects the overall organizational performance as engaged teams perform effectively and efficiently. Leaders need to assert values among teams and organizations to get exceptional performance. Values can be used as a leading tool and as a motivational tool. Not only must the charismatic leader possess reference power, intellectual and communication skills, influence on followers, ethical conduct, and courage, but he or she should be able to manage the follower's emotions intelligently. Babcock-Roberson and Strickland (2010) suggested that a leader's primary function may be the management of emotions at work.

- *Building a trusting relationship with followers.* The relationship between followers and the team leader affects work outcome. A leader who motivates and empowers his team will get them engaged and effective employees, where they focus on the overall performance and efficiency of the organization. Opposite to a directive, controlling, micromanager who is only concerned about deadlines and how his or her team image is reflected to top management. According to Astrini (2019), trust in leaders is a critical element in motivating employees to perform beyond requirements.

- *Providing incentives to followers.* As mentioned above, some followers need external incentives such as monetary awards and recognition to be motivated. Some followers like to know their efforts and contributions to the organization positively influence organizational performance. Leaders should practice recognition of individual's achievement and team achievement.

The economic success of any organization depends on the employees' capabilities and motivation in performing their work tasks. The direct result of unmotivated employees is low performance, low loyalty, looking for another job, or simply leaving the organization. Sustainability leaders must understand the motivational factors to their followers and use them wisely.

As an example of motivating and rewarding employees for their hard work and dedication, St. John Properties, one of the well-known leading real estate companies in the Mid-Atlantic, in December 2019 gave its employees bonuses totaling $10 million. As a result, every one of the 198 employees received about $50,000 on average. This bonus was in addition to other company's benefits. In addition to its appreciation to its employees and treating them as valued-ends, St. John properties are committed to sustainable design and construction since they focus on energy conservation and water savings in addition to reducing material waste and other sustainability strategies. Moreover, St. John Properties contributed about $65 million to philanthropic causes (https://www.sjpi.com).

Endorse Innovation

Some challenges facing organizations in the new economic state are related to radical environmental changes, how organizations respond to them, and how fast and effective their response might be. Other challenges are related to market demands, technological advances, and product development. However, for organizations to survive competition, stay at the frontier of product or service development, and to have a more significant market share, organizations should foster a structure and a culture of innovation. Innovation in organizations is necessary for contemporary global markets, whether it is in products or processes, it provides a competitive edge for those organizations which foster and adopt policies and structures to support innovation. Innovation encompasses proactively and initiation of employees to take extra roles, voluntary work beyond normal activities, creativity and organizational citizenship. Innovations start with generating creative ideas and ends with implementing them or receiving feedback and implementing them. According to Dorenbosh et al. (2005), innovative work behavior is the process of problem recognition and idea generation followed by idea promotion in terms of communicating its specifics with leaders and peers and then idea realization and implementing the solution. Therefore, leaders should encourage employees, implicitly and explicitly, to be innovative, which requires the business environment to be motivating to promote effective outcomes beyond job requirements.

Innovation Process

There is a lack of understanding among operational leaders of the connection between innovation and organizational sustainability. Mathur and Dabas (2014) argued that creating sustaining organizations is impossible without innovation. They reported that 95% of analysts on Wall Street found that innovative companies gain more share price premium than less innovative companies (Mathur & Dabas, 2014). Therefore, innovation can be considered as a facilitating process towards organizational sustainability.

Leaders who promote innovation are drivers of creating and achieving organizational sustainability objectives. Gubrud et al. (2017) indicated that innovation is one of the attributes of a sustaining organization, especially innovation in information technology (IT) which supports collaboration, communication, and social knowledge. In addition, innovation can be considered a process towards advancement in products, processes, and procedures that can become more efficient, of better quality, less cost, or better performance.

Innovation is neither the start nor the end of a process; instead, it is a process by itself. According to McFadzean (1998), the innovation process starts with creativity, which requires leaders to create an environment for collaboration and effective communication. Creativity can be realized as looking at the problem from a different perspective and resulting in several practical ideas; once evaluated and tested, the best idea becomes a viable or saleable product or service. Market demands might influence innovation, where older products and services no longer meet efficiency needs, or competitors have developed newer products. Additionally, innovation might be an internal push from the research and development department. Finally, innovation should be a strategy for organizations to establish a competitive edge. Wonglimpiyarat (2012) considered Michael Porter (1980) most influential in innovative strategy as Porter put forward the basic competitive strategy based on resource usage. Based on this theory, an organization can cope with changing competitive environment through its capabilities.

Organizational capabilities come from a mixture of resources, technology, experiences, and relationships. Porter (1980) (as cited in Wonglimpiyarat, 2012) established the Five Forces approach for the strategic position. The competitive position model's five forces include external relations with suppliers, negotiating power of buyers, fears of new competitors, threats of substitute products or services, and competition among existing firms (Wonglimpiyarat, 2012). It is important to note that strategy does not provide a competitive advantage if it is not executed and left as a vision of a dreamer. Communication is the key ingredient to the successful delivery of innovative products quickly and efficiently. As stated above, a strategy will not be a reality without execution. Innovation can take many years and some inventions in certain products occur more frequently.

Managing Organizational Innovation

While some researchers consider innovation based on the competitive strategy of the firm's capabilities, others believe that the business environment with the organization, collaborative leadership, and motivations for innovation are the main requirements for leaders to lead organizational innovation. Additionally, innovation does not necessarily need to be a new product or service; it can be a new or modified component of a product, a new administrative or management practice, a new layout of systems and subsystems, or simply a new theory. Many innovative behaviors and initiatives may not become part of the organizational daily activities or business, which means not all innovations become sustained change. For this reason, innovation can be achieved through sustained change. Razavi and Attarnezhad (2013) identified two prominent approaches for managing organizational change, the organizational capability approach and the transformational leadership approach:

- The organizational capability approach to innovation views the firm as a production machine of innovation and requires investments to nurture and to enhance its own capabilities.

Under this approach, innovation is not the sole responsibility of the research and management department alone, but it should be explored, harnessed, and motivated in every corner of the organization and its environment. Leaders might need to reform the reward and motivation system to manage innovation using this approach. Additionally, leaders should welcome and encourage creativity and challenging ideas that might be considered not normal. Moreover, leaders should assure resources availability and access to all elements of the organization, encourage risk-taking and entrepreneurship. Organizations should scan the business environment regarding what competitors are doing, and what the market demands and involve their customers in learning future innovations and needs.

- The transformational leadership approach relies on the fact that transformational leadership positively influences organizational innovation, as reported by Gumusluoğlu and Ilsev (2009). As discussed in Chapter 3, transformational leaders are characterized by idealized influence attributes, idealized influence behaviors, inspirational motivation, intellectual stimulation, and individualized consideration. Therefore, it is obvious that transformational leaders possess the needed skills to bring innovation out of followers. Inspirational motivation means that leaders inspire followers to go beyond their duties and allow them to explore new ideas and take risks. Intellectual stimulation refers to leader's capacity to promote creativity and thinking-ability to become more effective and productive. Transformational leaders empower employees to and build their confidence and personal development. Additionally, transformational leaders seek flexible organizational structures to harness innovation and capabilities of all followers. Therefore, organizations invest in hiring and training their leaders to become transformational leaders.

Innovation remains a critical attribute of a sustaining organization (Gubrud et al., 2017), and in achieving sustainability objectives (Mathur & Dabas, 2014) because leaders for organizational sustainability are either innovative or foster innovation into organizational elements (Burns et al., 2015; Gubrud et al., 2017; Metcalf & Benn, 2013). Leaders who foster innovations should encourage followers to think creatively and re-evaluate tools and means to develop better methods of doing things, value their expertise and voice, and support and endorse followers' ideas.

While innovation is an important process towards achieving organizational sustainability objectives, not all managers consider it or give it proper attention. Hasan (2018) found that 64% of leaders have a *no* to minimal influence and do not encourage innovation. Whenever organizations find out their operational leaders do not encourage innovation, they must re-evaluate their policies, procedures, the reward and incentive system, and the type of leaders they have.

CHAPTER 8:
EMOTIONALLY INTELLIGENT

There are many cases where insensitive leaders could not relate to followers' personal or work-related emotional issues resulted in negative consequences, including office violence that are such extreme as shooting and killing coworkers or management persons. It takes a quick review of the report by the Federal Bureau of Investigation (FBI) on active shooting cases between the years of 2000 and 2018 ("FBI, Active Shooter," 2019), to realize the severity and devastating consequences of some cases of workplace violence. More profound research on some cases reveals that the violence was triggered by an argument, dissatisfaction by a leadership decision, discrimination, stress, frustration, anger, bullying behaviors, or other feelings. Similarly, we find other leaders who could not control their feelings, resulting in negative consequences. For example, some leaders cannot manage their feelings of anger, sympathy, or excitement about a specific football team or political party.

Emotions play a significant factor in our lives since they provide drivers for many of our behaviors. When we like others, we like to help them; when we love someone, we also love to make them happy and do almost whatever they ask for. On the other hand, when we get angry about someone, we do not like to speak with them or even see them. In the same sense, leaders for organizational sustainability are inspiring and emotionally intelligent (Senbel, 2015), as well as they are excellent in building relationships. Emotional intelligence is a behavior aspect of servant leadership per Liden et al. (2014) and of transformational leadership per Dajani and Mohamad (2016). This behavior requires leaders to develop their relationship with followers and emphasize the values of sympathy, emotional awareness, and care.

Emotional intelligence (EI) is the competency to comprehend and manage our feelings and the feelings of others to be able to inspire ourselves and manage our relationships with others (Ölcer et al., 2014). Daniel Goleman refers to this as EQ. Effective leaders inspire followers and create passion in them towards achieving envisioned goals. Therefore, EI is a critical element of effective leadership and is dependent on social skills. Similarly, Hasan (2018) found that 100% of participant leaders described methods to cope with their followers' emotional distress.

Unfortunately, many leaders and business managers ignore their emotional side and that side of their followers and get immersed in their tasks, as their belief is that they were hired only to make profits, to get things done. Many leaders believe they were not hired to deal with people's problems, or they might have the mindset of autocratic leaders, which implies *do what I say* with no chance for collaboration or dialogue with followers. This is a significant difference between sustainability leaders and other types of leaders. Organizational sustainability leaders are considered effective with excellent interpersonal and relationship-building skills.

What is Emotional Intelligence?

This book is about leadership. Sustainability has various dimensions and it addresses and has concerns about all forms of life. I have explained in previous chapters that leadership is about influencing others, and that sustainability is about the flourishing of all forms of lives, which include human welfare and wellbeing, as well as the environment and its constituents, in addition to a thriving economy. Therefore, leadership for achieving organizational sustainability objectives become reliant on leaders' social and emotional intelligence. Our care for other life forms originates from our sympathy and behaviors triggered by various feelings, emotions, and cognitions to support and conserve these lives, sometimes some politicians need to demonstrate emotions of care as a pre-qualifier for their positions. For example, empathy is considered a positive emotion, as clarified by Dietz and Kleinlogel (2014), which means walking in someone else's shoes to understand their feelings. In other words, empathy is to react positively by one individual to the perceived experience of another individual. On the other hand, sympathy is an emotional response of one individual to another individual's emotional condition or state (Dietz & Kleinlogel, 2014). Therefore, before you let go of an employee, you might want to imagine that situation on yourself (being empathetic). If you face an outraged employee, you might want to express your feelings of sorrow and concern about his or her situation, or you should support him or her in some way (being sympathetic).

Salovey and Mayer (1990) used the emotional intelligence concept, later propagated by other scholars. There is almost an agreement among scholars about the definition of emotional intelligence. However, Crowne et al. (2017) clarified that EI is an ability to observe, express, and understand emotions accurately, as well as to use feelings to process and manage thoughts and emotions in others and self. Therefore, EI is an ability and can be developed as a characteristic of individuals through training, education, mentoring, or role-modeling. Many scholars clarified that EI can improve individuals' and organizations' performance. For example, Mayer et al. (2016) indicated that individuals with higher EI levels have better interpersonal relationships than less emotionally intelligent individuals. Additionally, EI can be a problem solver and a motivational source. Emotional feelings can be expressed and recognized through facial expressions, attitudes, body language, and behaviors towards tasks, others, and the organization. Therefore, leaders should develop their skills of EI to recognize and manage emotions in themselves and others.

At the beginning of my career, one of my mentors recommended a strategy to deal with controversy at work before responding to it, which is to *sleep on it*. One night or taking sufficient time to understand and process the agitating, aggravating, or other feelings triggered by others will help manage how we can respond wisely and professionally without escalating the issue to reflect negative consequences. Responding to controversy or disturbing comments from others can be fueled by anger, defense, or denial. As a result, responding can propagate into a problem instead of a solution and common understanding of the issue at hand.

Emotional distress is one of the significant factors driving low performance or/and employee separation from organizations. Leaders for organizational sustainability need skills in managing emotions appropriately in their organizations (Metcalf & Benn, 2013). Leaders can use transformational leadership or servant leadership strategies to manage the emotional distress of followers. Hasan (2018) found that most leaders use servant leadership elements as an emotional healer to manage followers' emotional distress. Leaders should try to understand the reasons behind the distress and help their followers since they care about them. Servant leaders are known to be emotional healers (Beck, 2014; Liden et al., 2014). However, when leaders prefer not to deal with follower's emotional distress, are challenged by it, or when they lack the skills in doing so, there should be an organizational assistance program that they can refer the follower to once they express distress.

Emotional Intelligence and Effective Leadership

Effective leadership has many inputs or facets, one of which is emotional intelligence. With the increase of competition in markets due to globalization and technological advances, organizations look for strategies to increase their effectiveness and market share. Research documented that employees and the workforce are the driving engines of production in organizations. Therefore, it is critical for leaders to understand employees' drivers and obstacles to support the former and decrease the latter for better organizational performance. Some researchers such as Bandi and Chauhan (2019) stated that EI of leaders and employees is necessary to encounter changes and to achieve organizational goals. In Chapter 3, I mentioned that intellectual stimulation and inspirational motivation can increase employee creativity, commitment, productivity, and organizational citizenship.

These contributions from employees and leadership skills can be based on the EI of leaders. To motivate and stimulate followers, leaders must allow them to express their thoughts and feelings freely which is one of the basics of EI. Additionally, in the previous chapter, I thoroughly described efficient leaders and explained that they cut production or service costs to increase profitability. However, some researchers such as Cotelnic and Timbaluic (2018) suggested that efficient leadership measures could include the attitude of followers towards their leader and towards each other, which can increase employee retention. An efficient leader can easily understand his or her followers' emotional status and interfere with directing or readjusting those emotions towards productivity by dealing effectively with followers' emotions. Leaders should understand that employees of the new age (Gen Z and Millennials) have different demands from the past century. Gen Z denotes individuals born between the years 1995 and 2010, while Millennials are born between 1980 and 1995. The new generation of followers has grown in an accelerating technological age, ever-changing environments, and an open and diversified world pushed by globalization. Therefore, the demands of the new generation of followers can be of autonomy and independence, but leaders should be involved, provide coaching, and use effective communication to clarify their expectations.

Additionally, new generational demands can be of having an opportunity for career advancement, but they might want that advancement quickly and within a few years of employment. For example, in the engineering field, where many employees work on designing and constructing buildings, it is common to provide a career advancement after 5 years of employment after graduating from college; however, it takes up to 10 years to build a professional, expert, and independent engineer. Other industries might have different advancement commonalities.

Moreover, the new generation of followers might need to be part of decision-making and recognized for their inputs.

The correlation between EI and leadership effectiveness can be explained by the fact that EI leaders are aware of their followers' emotions and able to deal with and regulate those emotions reflects on employees' organizational citizenship behaviors (OCB), organizational culture, employee performance, and counterproductive work behavior (CWB) reduction (Dirican & Erdil, 2019; Supramanian & Singaravelloo, 2019). In many cases of management practices, employees are promoted from technical positions to administrative and leadership positions with no to minimal knowledge of leadership and management skills and qualities. Sustainability leadership requires advanced management skills, strong personal qualities, and strong technical knowledge. Specifically, for the social dimension of sustainability which is frequently overlooked in organizations for the sake of the environmental and economic dimensions. While EI is a driving factor of effective leadership which might be present or not in leaders, it is a critical and main factor of leadership in specific fields such as healthcare, as noted by Stoller (2013), police departments, armed-forces divisions, and many others.

There are four dimensions for the ability model of EI as clarified by Dirican and Erdil (2019) and was previously formulated and updated in the work of Mayer et al. (2016). The first dimension is the ability to deal with self-emotions, understanding and expressing them. You have probably been or someone else has been in a situation where the manager acted angrily, sounded stressed, or with unwelcome behavior due to specific personal or business issues. Most of us, if not all, prefer that our managers control those negative emotions and somehow redirect them for better performance. Often, leaders' emotions resonate within followers and influence their emotional state, which in turn influences their productivity and performance.

The second dimension is the ability to observe emotions in others and recognize them. A leader with this ability can be empathetic, supportive, encouraging, and sensitive to others' feelings. This type of leader is usually *close* to their followers and can easily build trust-based and binding relationships with them. The third dimension is the ability to direct emotions to enhance performance. For example, a leader with EI perceives stress in one of his or her employees, then allows the follower to take an hour break, go to the gym, or even allow for early release for that follower (depending on the situation and perception). When the follower comes back to work, they will feel better and potentially refreshed with a better attitude towards work. The fourth dimension is the ability of leaders to regulate their emotions. It is about the leader's ability to mitigate negative feelings and return to normal psychological state.

Emotional Intelligence and Organizational Citizenship

The most significant influence of leaders' EI and followers' EI within an organization is increasing organizational commitment and organizational citizenship behaviors (OCB). Commitment of followers can be reflected in defense of their membership and association with the organization, which means followers are proud, satisfied, and persuaded by their organization's mission, vision, and services or products. Additionally, commitment can be reflected in followers' intention of their membership continuation of the organization. Recruiters find it difficult to recruit a committed follower to leave their organization to join another. Committed followers are the greatest asset an organization can have. Servant leaders can be considered emotionally intelligent since they care for their followers and participate in solving their problems. Perkasa and Abadi (2019) found that servant leadership behaviors such as being an active participant in solving follower's problems are significantly related to OCB and building good relationships with them incites OCB. Similarly, they found that the EI of followers is positive and significantly influences OCB.

Another research study conducted by Korkmaz and Arpaci (2009) found that leader's EI is positively related to followers' awareness, public engagement, and altruism, which are considered OCBs. For example, when followers feel understood, cared about, and appreciated, they become motivated and committed to their organization. Moreover, followers who get appreciation and motivation from their leaders will feel as if they belong to their organization, which is the basis for OCB. On the other hand, when leaders leave followers to resolve their own problems, whether professional or personal, they feel disengaged and not cared for. This becomes a trigger for followers to look for another organization to join that cares more about them, lowers their OCBs, and performance.

Emotional Intelligence and Service Delivery

In organizations, service delivery to customers is the main element in generating profits and financial performance and an excellent opportunity to interact with customers and clients to sustain them. Actually, some types of organizations can be extremely dependent on service delivery such as banks, restaurants, retail shops, hotels, and much more. In this type of organization, customer service and customer satisfaction might be the sole element in their survival. Therefore, leaders in such organizations should strive to improve service delivery through followers who interact with customers. For example, suppose that we want to realize the importance of service delivery. In that case, we can recall the times that we might have tipped a waiter generously for their great attitude and service, or decided not to return to a hotel we stayed in during our vacation due to the lack of timeliness in cleaning our rooms, or we might have posted a comment of a car dealership's site indicating they were crooks and cheaters because they might have cheated us in the interest rate on the loan or the vehicle itself.

With the increase in a global competition and decreased market share of organizations, customer retention becomes critical to organizational survival and performance. It is believed that there is a relationship between EI and the way leaders treat their followers of fairness and service delivery. Ashari et al. (2020) concluded that EI is positively but not significantly related to the quality of service through OCB, which can result in customer satisfaction and retention. Danquah and Wireko (2014) found that EI significantly affects customer service delivery and customer satisfaction in a different study. A service-based organization such as banks, which was the subject of the Danquah and Wireko study, EI is more important and significant in delivering service than other types of organizations. Since service deliver is based on interacting with customers, social skills become critical in enhancing followers' service delivery.

Emotional Intelligence and Performance

Many factors affect job performance such as leadership effectiveness, EI, satisfaction, organizational culture, commitment, and knowledge, skills, and abilities of followers known as KSA. Performance measurements are different for each organization; some organizations' performance measurement might be increasing productivity, improving quality, and attaining more customers, while others might be reducing costs, teamwork, and clear communication. Shahhosseini et al. (2012) clarified that EI has great power to explain followers' and organizational performance. EI can promote the creativity of individual followers and enhance effective communication (Shahhosseini et al., 2012), which might be considered the basis for performance. Emotions significantly influence one's decisions and behaviors in any situation, which means that managing one's or others' emotions properly will also influence their performance. Therefore, it becomes critical for leaders to understand and improve followers' welfare and living standards to reduce their emotional distress and improve their productivity. Leaders should strive to understand their followers' emotions and predict their behaviors in different situations using EI skills (Vanitha et al., 2020). Additionally, leaders should increase the level of EI of their followers because followers should understand the goals of their organizations and the emotions of their leaders. While organizations as business entities do not have emotions or feelings, their leaders do; this adds another level of emotional intelligence within organizations. Human Resources Management as a separate department within organizations should be at the forefront for EI skill development of leaders and followers.

Emotional Intelligence and Creativity

Researchers have long documented the significant role of creativity in sustainable development, including Xu et al. (2019). In any business organization, followers are the closest to the field since they perform production or service tasks daily. Therefore, their pioneering ideas at workplace about products, services, practices, or procedures can substantially contribute to organizational innovation, performance, effectiveness, and sustainability. Consequently, organizational leaders must identify factors and strategies that increase followers' creativity. Malik and Akhtar (2017) clarified that some factors are intrinsic, support, leadership style, and working environment. An emotional response to any situation or issue can vary from person-to-person and from time-to-time; however, the emotional response usually results in either positive or negative emotions. Moreover, Malik and Akhtar mentioned that research concluded that both negative and positive emotions significantly influence creativity.

While positive emotions can create an affective state that can enable creativity, and most of us clearly understand that positive emotions can lead to creativity, but not negative emotions. For example, let's assume a follower is exposed to a tedious procedure to create a business travel request which creates negative feelings of wasting time, dullness of procedure, and frustration with the system's bureaucracy. This perceived negative emotion about the travel procedure will trigger the creative mind of the follower to challenge this adverse effect and activate change-oriented thinking to find a more accessible and more exciting procedure. Sustainability leaders should be careful about relying on negative emotions to trigger creativity. They should study the overall organizational environment and understand the motivations of their followers and the level of their EI.

In Chapter 8, I clarified that creativity is the start of innovation and its bedrock. Gupta and Bajaj (2017) indicated that creativity is critical for organizations to deal with a complex and changing environment. Followers with emotional competency can detect and understand their emotional status and control it to lead them towards creativity. Leaders with EI should find ways to allow followers to understand and increase their EI to become creative.

The following strategies can be used to enable leaders in addressing and practice EI at business organizations:

- Leaders should strive to improve the level of their followers' EI by training and education, as suggested by Perkasa and Abadi (2019).

- Leaders should practice transformational leadership style or servant leadership style to address followers' issues.

- Leaders can practice transactional leadership style by not engaging in followers' issues; however, in this case, leaders should contract with a consultant so followers can refer to in solving their problems and issues.

- Leaders should build positive relationships with followers using effective communication.

- Leaders should increase followers' involvement in business issues, as described in the work of Cotelnic and Timbaliuc (2018).

- Leaders should monitor their own behaviors and attitudes, understand those of their followers (Modassir & Singh,

2008), and control their own feelings of fear, anger, and nervousness.

As presented in the previous discussions, EI is considered to have a critical influence on individuals, organizations, and societies. EI can be used to identify and train effective leaders. Emotionally intelligent leaders and followers are deemed to positively affect organizational sustainability including others they touch in their daily lives. Organizational upper leaders should consider EI to be a main facet of organizational setup. They can improve the level of this facet in their front-line leaders and followers by education and training.

CHAPTER 9:
ETHICAL, CHARACTERIZED BY INTEGRITY

Many researchers agree that the values of leaders drive their decisions and behaviors. For example, Florea et al. (2013) considered that values drive behaviors at personal and professional levels, in personal life and business settings. A leader's values have significant influences on their decision-making. Leaders with higher levels of moral development will make ethical decisions and will behave morally. A leader's morality does not only mean meeting organizational goals and complying with stated rules and policies without regard to follower needs and interests. Leaders with high morality have obligations towards their followers and organizations and treat their followers as valued ends, not as resources to create efficient organizations or generate profits (Caldwell et al., 2015).

Researchers emphasize that ethical leadership is linked to organizational sustainability and that ethical leaders do the right thing. Ethical leaders are characterized by values such as honesty, openness, trustworthiness, fairness, and integrity, and they do what is right. Virtue ethics are necessary to achieve sustainability and to shape attitudes towards sustainability. Therefore, it is clear that ethics are the foundation for sustainability because sustainability is an ethical and moral obligation because sustainability is linked to social justice and human and environmental development.

To understand how or why unethical behaviors continue to surface in organizations, we should explore two significant reasons:

- There are many situations that arise when organizational ethical norms are in conflict with ethical hyper-norms, as argued by Skubinn and Herzog (2016). In such situations, leaders fail to deliver favored results if they lack moral identity or when organizational ethics and personal ethics conflict. Examples of such situations include the need for spontaneous decisions during unexpected problems or emergency situations, or behaviors in defense of organizational survival or ethics regardless of negative consequences. A leaders' internalized moral identity enables them to produce positive deviant behavior in critical situations when tension between organizational ethics and good universal values exists. The business environment can face sudden changes and unexpected situations that challenge leaders, especially in globalized organizations and unstable political or economic environments.

- In addition, many leaders who consider themselves ethical have an individualistic view or self-centered view of ethics. These leaders are honest, kind, fair, and transparent in their personal life and with their community members but behave differently or opposite to those principles at work. Since leaders, like everyone else, are influenced by an idol who is a role model, be it a prophet, a philosopher, or a world leader, then why do many leaders separate their moral behavior in their personal conduct from business conduct?

Business competition is high, and technology continually advances, which presents more challenges to leaders. Business ethics, personal ethics, and universal ethics combined with contextual complications and challenges can drive an ethical person to do unethical behaviors. Let's take a look at the following imaginary scenarios where ethical dilemma arises:

Scenario 1: Assume there is an executive leader at a big publicly traded corporation, and the stock price of their corporation has been plummeting lately. At the end of the financial year, they win a contract of $100 million, but that will only cover expenses of employees, products, liabilities etc., with no profit. A middle manager approaches this leader and whispers "we can pay the product supplier $20 million in cash and that won't show up in the financial records. Therefore, the final financial reports will show a $20 million in profit." If the leader follows the middle manager's advice, their company's stock price will increase and potentially more people will buy into their corporation. Assume it is legal to do so. Eventually, they will be able to save the corporation and its reputation, sell stocks at a higher price, and potentially become rich. As an organizational sustainability officer, what do you suggest the leader do? Why?

Scenario 2: Assume a project leader is on a new building construction project. One of the subcontractors they have worked with successfully many times in the past wants to work on the new project, but the leader's company announced publicly soliciting for subcontractors. The subcontractor who previously worked with the leader visits the leader's house with a suitcase filled with $100,000, so the project leader will do their *magic* to make it appear that the subcontractor won the contract of their trade through the normal process of evaluation. This subcontractor is good at what they do and had proven records of successful work, will perform excellent on the new project, and no one will ever suspect anything. As an organizational sustainability officer, what do you suggest the leader do? Why?

Scenario 3: A leader is working in a chemical plant located in the North Country close to a river on the border with the South Country. One of the plant's production line processes is to collect chemical waste, encapsulate it, and box it for shipment to another waste treatment plant. The machine that processes waste for shipment is broken, will cost $100,000 to fix it, and it consumes electricity worth $50 per day to operate. The operator of this machine suggests to the leader that they could dump the waste into the river, saving the maintenance and the electricity costs. The savings look attractive, and the leader can renew other machines. The North Country will not be affected by the water pollution since the river runs to the South Country. As an organizational sustainability officer, what do you suggest the leader do? Why?

Corporations not only are legal entities, but also as members of societies, in which they operate, with responsibilities for human, economic, and social development. Additionally, organizations can have the flexibility to operate beyond the restricted legalities among countries. While the United States might have political issues with Russia, we can find American organizations operating in the heart of Moscow. By implementing policies, codes of ethics, and culture; corporations can affect employees' attitudes, education, and behavior in a positive way to support sustainable world objectives. Therefore, organizations can play a significant role in solving the sustainability problem. The primary determinant of ethical action is in the hands of leadership not in legislation. It is the leader's character that determines the action to be ethical or non-ethical. The leader's ethical character affects the employees' decisions and actions and consequently their ethical behavior.

What Do Ethical Values Mean?

Ethics may be considered as behavioral standards for an individual, a group, a society, or an organization by which behaviors of an individual, group, organization, or society members are judged. However, organizational ethics should comply and be in tandem with society's ethics. Otherwise, it will be rejected and negatively affected. Ethics are a combination of one's views of the outside world, and they are a mix of religious teachings, cultural norms, values and morals, and philosophical views. This is one reason for different views of ethics within the international community; what might be considered unethical in the United States might be considered ethical or business norms in China. And what might be considered ethical to one person might be considered unethical to another. Ethical decisions and behavior are not judged solely by that decision or action but by other constituents. There should be a baseline for what we might consider ethical action or not. This baseline involves the results or the consequences of the action, whether the results are harmful in any way to anyone or anything or the level of harm and the number of people / things affected by the behavior.

Additionally, the baseline of ethical behavior involves the intention of the action. For example, we often intend good deeds by our behaviors while the results can be against or different from to our intentions. Moreover, the ethical baseline of behaviors involves the consistency of the behavior with ethical norms and standards, i.e., does the behavior or decision comply with what others expect?

There are uncountable cases where confusion arises about a decision or a behavior, whether it is illegal or ethical. For example, is it ethical to lie or to steal to save one's life? Is it ethical for an unemployed pregnant woman to exaggerate on her resume to get a job so she can save her baby? On the other hand, many cases might be legal but unethical. For example, is it ethical for a private organization manager to hire his or her close relative while another candidate is more qualified? Is it ethical for a senator, whom the people have selected, to reject a notion against a poisonous or harmful product because the producing company contributed lots of money towards his candidacy? Ethics may be considered as the compass for the best behavioral direction among many other directions.

There are two major views of ethics: the relativist or individualism and the universal views. The relativist view or individualism refers to a self-orientation, an emphasis on self-sufficiency and control, the quest for individual goals that may or may not be consistent within-group goals, a willingness to challenge the in-group members, and a culture where people derive pride from their accomplishments (Morris et al., 1994). The relativist view of ethics believes what is right or wrong, is situational or dependent upon the culture, while the universal view of ethics believes in using the same standards in ethical judgment regardless of situation or culture.

What is Ethical Leadership?

Upper-level leaders in organizations can steer the organization towards its grave or toward the skies, and can influence its employees' lives, fate, and financial returns. Upper-level leaders can influence the environment and its resources. Additionally, influential leaders can advance their own economic status at the expense of their followers and their organization's interests. Moreover, leaders can use their formal power to abuse employees or mistreat and humiliate them. Some leaders can be abusive to their followers in a way that results in less loyal and less productive employees. This abusive behavior can result in increased unethical behaviors of employees, eroding trust between leaders and employees, and creating a toxic business culture.

There are many companies in which top leaders have been involved in unethical behaviors in the past years. Enron, Global Crossing, HealthSouth, Qwest, AIG, Tyco International, Fannie Mae, and WorldCom (Giroux, 2008) are only a few examples of those companies. The failure in most of these companies was recognized as both leadership failure and ethical failure (Allahar, 2021). The CEO and many executives of Enron had significant positions of power and influence but did not align their interests with the rest of the stakeholders, including employees. They actually preferred profits over ethics and displayed interest in hiding terrible news (Giroux, 2008). The CEO and many executives at Enron created an illusion of ethics and good culture, but the reality was ugly where charges included frauds in accounting reports and corruption (Edwards et al., 2019). Falsifying information about return on investments (ROI), creating subsidiaries that did not exist, and the persistence profit generation without restrains are a few of the unethical behaviors noted from scandals in many organizations. Unethical behavior can be very costly to organizations, and thus, punishment should prevent unethical behavior by others. People want to see social justice is retained and punishment is balancing actions of violations. Many scholars refer to the collapse of Enron as a result of failure in leadership ethics. Edwards et al. (2019) indicated that Enron employed close to 20,000 people and had revenues of $200 billion in 2000 but filed for bankruptcy in 2001.

There were a few signals of unethical behaviors that Fannie Mae ignored, which caused the organization's failure ethically and then financially. The board of directors tied its incentive plans to earnings per share (EPS), which caused a conflict of interest since the board was internal to the organization and none of the board members was external or independent. In other words, Fannie Mae's executives paid themselves big bonuses using overstated earnings (Yallaparagada, 2007). The individualism approach to ethics governs such board culture, where the focus is on self-interests. Additionally, Fannie Mae kept some financial records off the books, such as gains and losses on risky derivatives. The impact of these losses was found to be in multibillion-dollar figures; as Giroux (2008) mentioned, the frauds in their accounting practices were $16 billion. Even though financial principles can accept earnings management, it is not accepted by Generally Accepted Accounting Practice (GAAP).

It is helpful to see how much an organization earns before taxes, interests, and other financial deductions, however, it is vital to report actual earnings. Investors trust that the board of directors will manage their money and report the organization's performance effectively and transparently. The earnings management was tied to the incentive program of executives, and thus they made every effort to maximize the earnings per share (EPS), overlooking and ignoring many financial figures. While these errors may not be purposeful, the quality of reporting and the reliability of controls over the financial reporting process are questionable (Kalbers, 2009). Inaccurate financial reports signal incompetency and lack of integrity in the management system and the control system. Even though, an incorrect financial report might follow the law, it reflects manipulation of the system to meet required outcomes and does not reflect actual performance. From the writer's point of view, it is unethical behavior and has terrible outcomes on investors, creditors, suppliers, customers, employees, the government, and society.

Unfortunately, Enron's case was not the last one representing unethical behaviors by leaders. Unethical behaviors from organizational leaders continue to occur, as explained by Friedman and Gerstein (2016), since many organizations continue to sell dangerous products to consumers, including medicine or fabricated financial reports to maximize profits.

The research concludes that ethical leadership is distinguished from other leadership forms or theories of leadership by its ethical component, which has two aspects: the moral person aspect (personal character) and the moral manager aspect (business character). The moral person aspect includes the attributes of the ethical leader such as honesty, fairness, trustworthiness, integrity, empathy, and behaving ethically in personal life. On the other hand, the moral manager aspect includes that an ethical leader emphasizes ethics in the workplace and acts as a role model in conducting business matters for their followers. Therefore, ethical leadership is character-based or trait-based and behavioral-based.

The aspects of ethical leadership are apparent in the definition of ethical leadership as it has been first conceptualized and theorized in the past decade. Ethical leaders are considered role models for their followers because they are credible and legitimate through their own ethical actions and values. Additionally, ethical leaders use ethical decision-making, communication, and rewards and punishment to reinforce ethical standards within an organization. Moreover, ethical leaders create or change organizational culture and business environment to become a value-based culture, and they influence their followers to embrace ethical values. Brown et al. (2005) expressed that the appropriate behavior is context-based behavior, because appropriate behavior is based on the culture within which it is practiced. Context can be organizational or societal culture, job context and tasks, role definition, standards of conduct, and expected outcomes.

The development of ethical leadership is gradual and takes long years of experience, which shapes the leader's character. Nevertheless, ethical leaders should demonstrate certain ethical values, behaviors and motives. We can conclude from many studies conducted by many researchers such as Marsh (2013), Brooks and Normore (2005), Hasan (2018), and others, that the experience that shapes the ethical view of leaders towards life might consist of all or parts of the following:

- Experience with the external environment, i.e., the society.

- Experience and encounters with diversity. Encounters with different beliefs, philosophies, and views, encounters with different societies, and different or opposite values.

- Experience with difficult situations such as trauma, emergency situations, and ethically-critical situations.

- Experience with role models and mentors.

- Experience as the target of unethical behavior.

The development of the leader's character results in a choice to lead ethically, and hence ethical leadership is based on the moral development of the leader.

Business Ethics

Business ethics are not clearly defined in a global market or an international view as one set of ethical principles, which can be applicable anywhere. For example, what can be considered ethical in America might be considered unethical in Japan. Ethics from one country to another vary as the origins of ethics are cultural and socially related. Additionally, business ethics are different from individual ethics because what might be considered ethical behavior by individuals, which is not immoral or illegal, might be considered unethical behavior if done by business such as the submission to extortion or favoritism. For example, on an individual level, favoring one's son or daughter in many ways is considered ethical and probably encouraged socially and culturally in many countries. However, favoritism in job hiring or promotions can be considered unethical in many private and public organizations.

Business ethics should be universal and more committed by higher ranked people in the organization and are the same for all. Since we are humans and are interconnected with shared resources, have similar ambitions, and suffer similarly from unethical behaviors. Business ethical behavior should be judged on how it contributes to the common good of all of us and the living species on Earth. However, we all want and expect the products we buy to be worth our money and have the qualities and features as advertised on the label or by the manufacturer. We all want and expect the selling company to honor its contract of warranty if the product we buy malfunctions or is damaged. We all want and expect respect and to be treated with kindness and with kindness when we interact with sales personnel and staff members. In many cases, we trust physicians with our lives in healthcare organizations, so we expect they do their best to save us and do the best for us. Because simply we are the customer, we are the reason companies exist. And if a particular company does not meet those expectations, it most likely they won't exist for a long time.

Responsibility is a core principle of business ethics, and thus, if a business is said to be ethical, it has to be responsible. The responsibility of a person or a business corporation means having the ability to respond to a situation, issue, or another action done by others. It is a moral obligation, and thus, the business is responsible for the environment and the society it acts within. Any business organization has obligations to society and the environment, in addition to its employees which is called the social responsibility of the organization. The minimal ethical obligation of any organization is its legal responsibility of abiding by the law. Additionally, organizations should be obligated towards the fair treatment of employees, customers, and suppliers, and building trustworthy and transparent relationships. Those in high leadership levels should have the greatest responsibility.

How are Ethical Values Linked to Sustainability?

Scholars have no agreement on what specific ethical values are required most in an ethical leader, and there are different views of ethical leadership. To establish a connection between ethical leadership (context-based) and sustainability (universal-based), we ought to find and integrate the driving philosophies of ethics. It might be impossible to find a leader who admits that their actions or the results of their actions are unethical because they adopt different ethical philosophies that guide their behaviors. This section contains a review of the most common ethical theories:

A review of philosophical theories of ethics shows debate and contradiction about what and how to achieve human good life or happiness. *Deontological* or *Altruism* ethics by Kant (1781) considered the action itself to be either right or wrong without considering its consequences. The only motive to goodwill is the duty (Kant, 1959). In other words, morality and moral actions should stem from a sense of duty, meaning a person should feel it is their duty to do something moral. This view does not consider the consequences of actions. Moreover, Kant believed that the principles of an action should have universal meaning and helping others should be grounded in universal law. For example, based on Kant's (1959) philosophy, what power companies did in the past was moral by providing power regardless of the environmental consequences and pollution. Additionally, when universalized particular rules become inconsistent, they become immoral. However, adhering to sustainability requirements of social justice, environmental development, and economic development can be viewed as the duty of leaders in organizations. Therefore, sustainability has a duty-based element.

Utilitarianism or *teleological* ethics developed by Jeremy Bentham (1748-1832) and John Stewart Mill (1806-1873), considers a behavior right or wrong by its consequences, and not on its motives, and that the action brings happiness or goodness to a greater number of people. The utilitarian approach considers the outcome and excuses the means (Bentham, 1982; Mill, 1962). For example, under the utilitarian approach, a leader can lie or fabricate their company's financial reports to justify the company's survival. Under sustainability lens, the consequences of fostering sustainability in one's organization will contribute to the universe's well-being and brings happiness to all life forms on Earth. Therefore, sustainability has a utilitarian element.

Virtue ethics are not led by rules or consequences but by developing the virtuous person to do good. Aristotle is the father of this theory, a Greek philosopher, lived in the Fourth Century B.C. (384-322 B.C). Aristotle (1999) emphasized developing the virtuous human being to achieve good or happiness. Aristotle was concerned with the character of the people, not their actions, rules, laws, or consequences. He based the end of achieving humans' goal of happiness, on the virtuous character, which is driven by virtues. It becomes evident the relationship between sustainability and Aristotle's theory.

Flourishing life on Earth requires virtuous leaders driven by virtue values. Transformational leadership correlates to deontological ethics, while transactional leadership correlates to utilitarian ethics (Groves & LaRocca, 2011). Additionally, Caldwell et al. (2015) clarified that virtuous leaders recognize the need to serve others, make decisions to help their organizations, create a better world for future generations, and are motivated by service, excellence, and responsibility. Therefore, virtuousness encompasses servant leadership. Astrini (2019) documented that leaders can gain followers' trust by emphasizing servant leadership behaviors which is critical for increased organizational citizenship behavior. Moreover, Asrori and Muslichah (2018) found that trust-in-leader (TIL) is a positive and significant effect of transformational leadership. According to Stedham and Skaar (2019), TIL is a critical element in leadership effectiveness and motivating followers to perform beyond requirements.

Leadership for organizational sustainability is value-driven and should focus on universal ethics such as integrity, trust, transparency, care, fairness, and honesty. Moreover, leadership for organizational sustainability should have a long-term perspective and global responsibility to serve a more significant cause. Communication and building relations with followers are a few skills that leaders for organizational sustainability should have, in addition to their ability to generate profits to justify their organization's existence and to be able to support other business functions. Other skills include monitoring work progress and solving problems (Williams & Turnbull, 2015), they should be emotionally intelligent and inspire others (Senbel, 2015), and they should be experts in building strong relationships with all stakeholders.

Therefore, leaders for organizational sustainability are efficient managers who value the continuation of their organizations through generating financial profits, value individuals and their needs within their organizations, and are versed to serve a greater good. Additionally, leadership style and organizational culture are critical elements for the success and performance of organizations (Puni & Bosco, 2016). Leadership effectiveness is dependent on cultural values within the organization (Puni & Bosco, 2016). Therefore, leaders must instill a culture of integrity and values for organizational sustainability.

The ethical approach to sustainability supports organizational sustainability and provides a clear understanding of decisions regarding sustainability practices as some companies consider sustainability practices part of their code of conduct. Vinkhuyzen and Karlsson-Vinkhuyzen (2014) found that the ethical dimension of leadership adds value to the potential leadership style needed for the change towards sustainability. The characteristics of the moral leadership model that Vinkhuyzen et al. (2014) established are: (a) serving the common good and (b) working towards personal and collective change. Moreover, this model is (c) servant not controlling, (d) humble, and (e) builds cohesive teams and efficient in executing tasks. Sustainability is an ethical and a moral obligation where sustainability relates to social justice, a moral obligation for human development, and a sustaining economy. McCann and Sweet (2014) concluded that sustainability leadership focuses on long-term thinking, the integrity of leaders is the paramount character of leaders, and ethical leadership and sustainability leadership are critical to the success of financial institutions. Therefore, the sustainability leadership construct has its basis on ethics and integrity as the primary drivers for sustainability leadership.

Organizational sustainability extends beyond the borders, policies, and operations of organizations; therefore, leadership should be able to capture the required responsibility and duties owed by their organizations towards the world. Peterlin (2016) clarified that leaders for organizational sustainability care for the individuals and the organization and extend that care for the environment and the world. Moreover, leaders for organizational sustainability should collaborate with internal and external stakeholders to create the change needed to transform their organization towards sustainability. Adherence and promotion of sustainability within an organization, government, or even individual level is a choice driven by values and beliefs. There might be regulations, laws, and standards, to govern some behaviors to restrict harm to the environment and social aspects of our lives. However, regulations, laws, and standards will not be able to dictate one's or philanthropic organizational policy, or recycling policy, or for one to take the bus to work rather than driving his or her car. Additionally, sustainability is a universal issue, where polluted air or contaminated water can travel through the borders of countries. Terrorism affects economies and the social life of many people throughout the world. Some environmental problems can extend through generations and through space and time. Therefore, ethical values as an enabling framework for sustainability should be universal. Behaviors that have their basis on values can make aspects of sustainability flourish and consequently the life on earth thrive. Therefore, organizational sustainability is driven and attained by value-based behaviors and actions.

Hasan (2018) concluded that the ethical values needed in a leader to achieve organizational sustainability objectives are virtue ethics (72%), deontological ethics (14%), and utilitarian ethics (14%). Virtue ethics align with servant leadership since virtuous leaders recognize the need to serve others, make decisions to help their organizations, create a better world for future generations, and are motivated by service, excellence, and responsibility (Caldwell et al., 2015). Transformational leadership correlates to deontological ethics and transactional leadership correlates to utilitarian ethics (Groves & LaRocca, 2011). Therefore, virtue or universal ethics are the most desired and required values in organizational sustainability leaders.

Integrity

Integrity is an essential ethical trait or character expected to be present in corporations and leaders to be ethical, responsible, and accountable. Integrity is the unity and integration of several moral values that are upheld and consistently practiced. In leadership, it represents highly ethical, responsible, and accountable leaders. When we refer to someone with integrity, we mean they are uncorrupted and resist temptations to sacrifice their moral values for self or other interests (Bauman, 2013). Leaders who behave with integrity not only have the interests of their followers, their organizations, but the society as a whole and the universe. There is also no agreement among scholars on what integrity means or what it involves (Monga, 2016; Veríssimo & Lacerda, 2015). In a review of five meanings of integrity; Monga (2016) proposed that integrity has an intrinsic dimension: the absolute obligation to sound ethical values and extrinsic aspects that are the reflection of these moral principles in behaviors and actions. However, some scholars viewed integrity as the absence of unethical behavior, and it is an ethical conduct. A leader's integrity remains a critical element of leadership, and it is an antecedent of effective and authentic leadership for sustainability.

The most accepted definition of integrity is that leader's integrity is the consistent moral behavior over time, in all situations, and the execution of promises in adherence to moral values of fairness, honesty, and respect. Integrity monitoring in government and private sector organizations that rely on transparency is an effective strategy to detect and prevent fraud, because of addressing problems before they occur (Donohue, 2015). However, integrity monitoring that depends on compliance with laws and regulation is ineffective since criminal or abusive minds can find a way to abuse their position and power. Legislation and regulations exist; however, financial and other types of fraud continue to surface. Laws and regulations in government agencies are firm and violating them can yield counterproductive practices and hinder morale and compromise the security and safety of employees, or the nation at large. The best monitoring method of integrity is self-guided integrity, where one is their monitor.

Views of Integrity

The research concludes that there are two views of integrity, the objectivist (moral) view and the normative (behavioral) view (Monga, 2016). Simons et al. (2015) indicated that behavioral integrity is different from moral integrity, and moral integrity is adherence to socially favorable values and acting in agreement with those values while behavioral integrity is the voice of leader's values regardless of ethical content.

- The *Moral (or Objectivist) Integrity* view defines integrity in the social context with no regard to the human emotions, biases, actions, or feelings; therefore, integrity is what others perceive a particular person to behave morally per socially-accepted principles and honor one's words. But how does this view align with the complexities of human and societal nature? Moral integrity is adherence to socially favorable values and acting in agreement with those values. Socially desirable values can be detrimental to organizations and might not contribute to the organizational sustainability of a sustainable World as a whole. Monga (2016) criticized this view as it neglects the subjectivity of the human nature. Genocide of non-Catholic Christians would be justifiable and considered ethical under this narrow definition of integrity because it was socially accepted to do in the history of the United States as the genocide of Mormons. Many other examples exist where *socially-accepted* values do not align with world's sustainability objectives. A small fraudulent group or criminals can create their own *socially-accepted* values; therefore, this view accepts their moral integrity.

- The *Behavioral (or Normative) Integrity* view defines integrity in several ways as consistently acting in agreement with virtues, consistency between words and deeds, authenticity, which means consistency between embraced values and behavioral values, and moral behavior in congruence with honesty, empathy, justice, respect, trustworthiness, and fairness. Behavioral integrity is essential to building trust in a leader, and it is an antecedent of courage, which is defending what is right regardless of opposition (Palanski et al., 2014). However, words and promises can be unethical; therefore, the context and consequences should be part of integrity judgment (Monga, 2016). Behavioral integrity is concerned with the leader's character and pattern of behavior reflecting a narrow context that deems those practices acceptable. Per this view, one can be considered behaving with integrity according to the entity's values they represent, whether it is an organization, small group, or community. However, this view accounts for personal integrity of commitment to words and promises and not necessarily moral integrity or pledge to values. Using this view, a mob's leader or an autocratic leader who executes commitments and promises can be considered as leader with integrity.

Operational leaders of organizational sustainability should be aware of the different views of integrity and should adopt what makes sustainability sense. In this review, I recommend that the integrity of a leader is their demonstration of commitment to universal ethical values in their conduct (personal and professional), in all contexts and situations, with consistency and continuity.

Benefits of Integrity

A leader's integrity is critical to the success of any organizational sustainability objectives. Imagine a leader sends a message to their employees asking them to ride the bus to work to reduce gas emissions while the leader drives an 8-cylinder vehicle; how does that reflect on the employee's perception? Leader's integrity has many benefits, but here are a few:

- Leaders' integrity can enhance organizational effectiveness because there is a positive link between integrity and different leadership styles such as servant, transformational, authentic, and ethical leadership style in addition to other styles. Therefore, integrity leads to a value-driven leadership style.

- Leaders' integrity creates credibility and trust in leaders (Engelbrecht et al., 2015). Trust in leaders is built on the moral behaviors of the leader and it increases the confidence of employees in their leaders and their decisions. Trust in leaders is a critical factor in motivating followers towards higher performance levels (Asenco & Mujkic, 2016).

- Leaders' integrity leads to effective interpersonal communication, executing promises to employees, and transparency enhancing trust in a leader. A leader's moral behavior causes employees to trust that leader, increases their work engagement, dedication, and contributes positively to organizational effectiveness (Chughtai et al., 2015).

- Leaders' integrity has a high correlation with reducing the likelihood of financial exploitations. Values of a leader have a trickle-down effect from leadership to employees, and the organization's financial future depends on the financial integrity of the leader (Hasan, 2018).

Organizational sustainability leaders should be characterized with integrity and ensure that their organizations have ethical values that align with sustainable world objectives and formulate the basis for decision-making. Those values must be practiced and manifested in all business elements of the organization. One of the reasons for organizational collapse is the neglect of ethical values in the daily life of organizations, primarily by leaders who engage in negative deviant behaviors.

Ethical Guidelines for Organizational Sustainability Leaders

It is worth mentioning that this chapter does not intend to portray business organizations as unethical but to reflect on the detrimental effects unethical behaviors by leaders can cause.

Business organizations contribute to the growth of the local and national economy; they produce products or provide services that benefit humans, contribute to our household income and daily living expenses, and contribute to the advancement of human knowledge. While there are many steps, strategies, or decisions a leader can take to enrich organizational culture with ethical values, the following are major ethical guidelines for organizational sustainability leaders:

- Create an organizational culture and business environment based on universal ethical values and moral behaviors.

- Create or modify a code of ethics for the organization to align with the values of world sustainability objectives such as honesty, fairness, trustworthiness, care, transparency, and respect.

- Organizational leaders should act as role models for their followers and do what they say or promise to do.

- Establish fair punishment strategies for unethical behaviors and fair reward strategies to recognize employees' performance in the ethics part of their overall performance.

- Create an annual ethical training for followers.

- Ensure compliance with ethical values adopted in the mission and values statement in all business facets, consistent, continuous, and in all situations.

- Organizations should not ignore any ethical problem within teams or the organization.

- Organizational leaders should encourage their followers to report any unethical or illegal behavior they suspect, make the reporting process confidential, and guarantee the reporter's safety as possible.

- Leaders should use effective communication to emphasize their organization's ethical message and mission to followers and other shareholders.

- Make ethics screening of potential hires as part of the hiring process.

In today's world, where information spreads at the speed of light, increased consumer awareness of right and wrong business practices, and increased competition, it is difficult for any organization to remain viable if the behaviors by its leaders and within its business transactions are unethical. Therefore, ethics and ethical leaders are indispensable for the success of organizational sustainability objectives. Organizational sustainability leaders must be cognizant of their values and behaviors and strive to align their personal and organizational values with universal values.

CONCLUSION

This book was written to provide a clearer understanding of the leadership behaviors and values needed in achieving organizational sustainability objectives and as a means to provide social justice and environmental development and the core business requirements of financial profits to help leaders be successful in their roles towards organizational sustainability.

While most organizational leaders today have some commitment to sustainability, they are still challenged by appropriate leadership style to adopt for the success of organizational sustainability objectives. While much has been written on sustainability and leadership, there is still a lack of information and research on the makeup of sustainability leadership and its construct. The recommendations of this book added to the existing literature on leadership and organizational sustainability. They have critical implications on leadership effectiveness because of the values and integrity influences. Additionally, the behaviors and attributes of the leadership style mapped based on the integrative approach employed in this book resulted in an integration of the leadership styles instead of relying on a single leadership style because a single leadership style is not sufficient to achieve organizational sustainability objectives. In contrast, the integrative approach is a better tool to do so.

The integrative approach employed serves as a theoretical

foundation to study leadership for organizational sustainability and a prescriptive plan to executives for selecting and training leaders for organizational sustainability. This integrative leadership approach might inspire more leaders to use the recommendations of this book to significantly enhance the success of leadership for organizational sustainability in different organizational environments. The application and the resultant leadership style in this study of the integrative approach of the transactional, transformational, servant, and ethical leadership theories is significantly affected by a leader's values and integrity.

Moreover, leadership for organizational sustainability is not clearly understood. Without this book, leaders of organizational sustainability are left to rely on traditional leadership styles, intuition, or employing one specific style, but may not find these styles adaptable or successful in achieving sustainability objectives, specifically as enablers against social injustice, financial exploitations, and environmental degradation. Sustainability is a complex and interdisciplinary issue, and it requires a different leadership style.

Organizational leaders should understand that sustainability is not a one-country issue or bound boundary issue but a global and progressive issue. Moreover, they should acknowledge that social; and environmental dimensions of sustainability are as crucial to the success of the organization as the financial dimension. Leaders should start by implementing continuous and meaningful sustainability changes to see tangible improvements in organizational sustainability performance. This book provided specific behaviors based on components and constructs of the four leadership styles used in the integrative approach and demonstrated that some components are not exclusively restricted to certain styles; therefore, leadership styles can be integrated to find new avenues of leadership.

We have witnessed several weather-related disasters, pandemic spread, floods, hurricanes, wildfires, and droughts in recent years. These challenges affected the environment, the financial growth of organizations and countries, and the mental and psychological state of employees and residents. Organizations contribute in many ways to the severity of these disasters and can contribute vastly to the solution of these problems.

REFERENCES

Agboola, A., & Salawu, R. (2011). Managing deviant behavior and resistance to change. *International Journal of Business & Management, 6*(1), 235-242. https://doi.org/10.5539/ijbm.v6n1p235

Allahar, H. (2021). Ethical behavior and leadership effectiveness. *Academia Letters*, Article 3528. https://doi.org/10.20935/AL3528

Ashari, I., Rakhmar, Allorante, A. I., & Ahmad, B. (2020). The effect of organizational justice and emotional intelligence on service quality through organizational citizenship behavior. *International Journal of Multicultural and Multirelegious Understanding, 7*(2), 287-293. https://doi.org/10.18415/ijimmu.v7i2.1494.

Asif, M., Miao, Q., Jameel, A., Manzoor, F., & Hussain, A. (2020). How ethical leadership influence employee creativity: A parallel multiple mediation model. *Current Psychology*. https://doi.org/10.1007/s12144-020-00819-9

Asrori, S. M., & Muslichah, M. (2018). The effect of transformational leadership style on job satisfaction with trust-in-leader as intervening variable. *Journal of Innovation in Business Economics, 2*(2), 61-70. https://doi.org/10.22219/jibe.v2i02.6580

Astrini, A. D. (2019). The effect of servant leadership on organizational citizenship behavior: The role of trust in leader as a mediation and perceived organizational support as a moderator. *Journal of Leadership in Organizations, 1*(1), 1-16.

Babcock-Roberson, M., & Strickland, O. (2010). The relationship between charismatic leadership, work engagement, and organizational citizenship behaviors. *Journal of Psychology, 144*(3), 313-326. https://doi.org/10.1080/00223981003648336

Bandi, S., & Chauha, N. (2019). Effect of emotional intelligence on employee performance. *ISBR Management Journal, 1*(4). https://isbrmj.org/index.php/home/article/view/56

Bass, B. M. (1990). From transactional to transformational leadership: Learning to share the vision. *Journal of Organizational Dynamics, 18*(3), 19-31. https://doi.org/10.1016/0090-2616(90)90061-S

Bate, P., Khan, R., & Pye, A. (2000). Towards a culturally sensitive approach to organization structuring: Where organization design meets organizational development. *Organization Science, 11*(2), 197-211.

Bateh, J., Heaton, C., Arbogast, G. W., & Broadbent, A. (2013). Defining sustainability in the business setting. *American Journal of Business Education (Online), 6*(3), 397.

Bauman, D. C. (2013). Leadership and the three faces of integrity. *The Leadership Quarterly, 24*, 414-426. http://doi.org/10.1016/j.leaqua.2013.01.005

Bodle, R., Donat, L., & Duwe, M. (2016). The Paris Agreement: Analysis, assessment and outlook. *Ecologic. German Federal Environment Agency (UBA) Research Paper.* http://ecologic.eu/sites/files/event/2016/ecologic_institute_2016_paris_agreement_assessment.pdf

Brooks; J. S., & Normore, A. H. (2005). An Aristotelian framework for the development of ethical leadership. *Journal of Rock Ethics Institute, 3*(2), 1-8. https://files.eric.ed.gov/fulltext/EJ1186506.pdfhttps://files.eric.ed.gov/fulltext/EJ1186506.pdf

Brown, M. E., Treviño, L. K., & Harrison, D. A. (2005). Ethical leadership: A social learning perspective for construct development and testing. *Organizational Behavior & Human Decision Processes, 97*(2), 117-134. https://doi.org/10.1016/j.obhdp.2005.03.002

Brown, H. S., & Vergragt, P. J. (2015). From consumerism to wellbeing: Toward a cultural transition? *Journal of Cleaner Production.* https://doi.org/10.1016/j.jclepro.2015.04.107

Bureau of Labor Statistics. (2020). *Assessing the impact of new technologies on the labor market: Key constructs, gaps, and data collection strategies for the Bureau of Labor Statistics.* https://www.bls.gov/bls/congressional-reports/assessing-the-impact-of-new-technologies-on-the-labor-market.htm

Burnes, B., & Jackson, P. (2011). Success and failure in organizational change: An exploration of the role of values. *Journal of Change Management, 11*(2), 133-162.

Bushardt, S. C., Glascoff, D. W., & Doty, D. H. (2011). Organizational culture formal reward structure, and effective strategy implementation: A conceptual model. *Journal of Organizational Culture, Communications and Conflict, 15(2)*, 57-70. https://www.abacademies.org/articles/joc-ccvol15no22011.pdf

Caldwell, C., & Hasan Z. (2016). Covenantal leadership and the psychological contract: Moral insights for the modern leader. *Journal of Management Development, 35*(10), 1302–1312. https://doi.org/10.1108/jmd-02-2016-0027

Carter, D., & Baghurst, T. (2014). The influence of servant leadership on restaurant employee engagement. *Journal of Business Ethics, 124*(3), 453-464. https://doi.org/10.1007/s10551-013-1882-0

Chountalas, P. T., & Lagodimos, A. G. (2019). Paradigms in business process management specifications: a critical overview. *Business Process Management Journal, 25*(5), 1040–1069. https://doi.org/10.1108/BPMJ-01-2018-0023

Chughtai, A., Byrne, M., & Flood, B. (2015). Linking ethical leadership to employee well-being: The role of trust in supervisor. *Journal of Business Ethics, 128*(3), 653-663. https://doi.org/10.1007/s10551-014-2126-7

Cooperrider, D., & Fry, R. (2012). Mirror flourishing and the positive psychology of sustainability. *Journal of Corporate Citizenship, 46*, 3-12. https://doi.org/10.9774/GLEAF.4700.2012.su.00002

Cotelnic, A., & Timbaliuc, A. (2018). Emotional intelligence and their role in managerial process. *Review of General Management, 27*(1), 74-85. http://www.managementgeneral.ro/pdf/1-2018-7.pdf

Crowne, K. A., Young, T. M., Goldman, B., Patterson, B., Krouse, A. M., & Proenca, J. (2017). Leading nurses: Emotional intelligence and leadership development effectiveness. *Leadership in Health Services, 30*(3), 217-232. https://doi.org/10.1108/LHS-12-2015-0055

Danquah, E., & Wireko. T. B. (2014). The impact of each element of emotional intelligence on customer service delivery: A customer satisfaction perspective. *International Journal of Sales & Marketing Management Research and Development, 4*(2), 9-20. http://www.tjprc.org/

Deschamps, C., Rinfret, N., Lagacé, M. C., & Privé, C. (2016). Transformational leadership and change: How leaders influence their followers' motivation through organizational justice. *Journal of Healthcare Management, 61*(3), 194-212. https://doi.org/10.1097/00115514-201605000-00007.

Dorenbosch, L., van Engen, M. L., & Verhagen, M. (2005). On-the-job innovation: The impact of job design and human resource management through production ownership. *Creativity & Innovation Management, 14*(2), 129-141.

Derue, D. S., Nahrgang, J. D., Wellman, N., & Humphrey, S. E. (2011). Trait and behavioral theories of leadership: An integrated and meta-analytic test of their relative validity. *Journal of Personnel Psychology, 64*(1), 7-52. https://doi.org/10.1111/j.1744-6570.2010.01201.x

Dervitsiotis, K. N., & Kanji, G. K. (1998). A new total quality management frontier: Getting ready to jump the curve. *Total Quality Management, 9*(4/5), s56-s61. https://doi.org/10.1080/0954412988569

Deutsch, N., & Pécs, U. (2013). Note on the development of sustainable supply chain strategy. *Chemical Engineering Transactions, 35*, 655-660. https://doi.org/10.3303/CET1335109

Dietz, J., & Kleinlogel, E. P. (2014). Wage cuts and managers' empathy: How a positive emotion can contribute to positive organizational ethics in difficult times. *Journal of Business Ethics, 119*(4), 461–472. https://doi.org/10.1007/s10551-013-1836-6

Dilling, P. F. A. (2010). Sustainability reporting in a global context: What are the characteristics of corporations that provide high quality sustainability -an empirical analysis. *The International Business & Economics Research Journal (IBER), 9*(1).

Dirican, A. H., & Erdil, O. (2019). The influence of ability-based emotional intelligence on discretionary workplace behaviors. *Journal of Human Behavior in the Social Environment.* https://doi.org/10.1080/10911359.2019.1687388

Djordjevic, A., & Cotton, D. R. E. (2011). Communicating the sustainability message in higher education institutions. *International Journal of Sustainability, 12*(4), 381-394. https://doi.org/10.1108/14676371111168296

Donohue, K. M. (2015). Combatting fraud, waste and abuse: A more proactive approach is the answer. *The Journal of Government Financial Management, 64*(1), 54-55.

Eccles, R. G., Perkins, K., & Serafeim, G. (2012). How to become a sustainable company. *MIT Sloan Management Review, 53*(4), 43-50. https://sloanreview.mit.edu

Edwards, G., Hawkins, B., & Schedlitzki, D. (2019). Bringing the ugly back: A dialogic exploration of ethics in leadership through an ethno-narrative re-reading of the Enron case. *Journal of Human Resources.* https://doi.org/10.1177/0018726718773859

Ehrenfeld, J. R. (2005). The roots of sustainability. *MIT Sloan Management Review, 46*(2), 23-23. https://sloanreview.mit.edu/article/the-roots-of-sustainability/

Ehrenfeld, J. R. (2012). Beyond the brave new world: Business for sustainability In P. Bansal & A. J. Hoffman (Eds.), *The Oxford handbook of business and the natural environment* (pp. 611-619). Oxford University Press. https://doi:10.1093/oxfordhb/9780199584451.003.0033

Elkington, R., & Upward, A. (2016). Leadership as enabling function for flourishing by design. *Journal of Global Responsibility, 7*(1), 126-144. https://doi.org/10.1108/JGR-01-2016-0002

Engelbrecht, A. S., Heine, G., & Mahembe, B. (2015). The influence of integrity and ethical leadership on trust in the leader. *Management Dynamics, 24*(1), 2-10. https://hdl.handle.net/10520/EJC168482

Federal Bureau of Investigation (FBI). (2019). *Active shooter incidents in the United States from 2000-2018.* https://www.hsdl.org/?abstract&did=834188

Ferdig, M. A. (2007). Sustainability leadership: Co-creating a sustainable. *Journal of Change Management, 7*(1), 25-35. https://doi.org/10.1080/14697010701233809

Friedman, H. H., & Gerstein, M. (2016). *Are we wasting our time teaching business ethics? Ethical lapses since Enron and the great recession.* https://doi.org/10.2139/ssrn.2839069

Geissdoerfer, M., Savaget, P., Bocken, N., & Hultink, E. (2017). The circular economy – A new sustainability paradigm? *Journal of Cleaner Production, 143*(1), 757-768. https://doi.org/10.1016/j.jclepro.2016.12.048

Giroux, G. (2008). What went wrong?: Accounting fraud and lessons from the recent scandal. *Social Research: An International Quarterly, 74*(4), 1205-1238. https://doi.org/1353/sor.2008.0026

Glavas, A., & Mish, J. (2015). Resources and capabilities of triple bottom line firms: Going over old or breaking new ground? *Journal of Business Ethics, 127*(3), 623-642. https://doi.org/10.1007/s10551-014-2067-1

Gubrud, P., Spencer, A. G., & Wagner, L. (2017). From start-up to sustainability: A decade of collaboration to shape the future of nursing. *Nurs-

ing Education Perspectives, 38(5), 225-232. https://doi.org/10.1097/01. NEP.0000000000000212

Gumusluoğlu, L., & Ilsev, A. (2009). Transformational leadership and organizational innovation: The roles of internal and external support for innovation. *Journal of Product Innovation Management, 26*(3), 264-277.

Gupta, R., & Baja, B. (2017). The relationship between leader's emotional intelligence and employee creativity: A conceptual framework of mechanism. *Information Technology and Quantitative Management (ITQM 2017)*, 471-477.

Hasan, Z., & Roach., J. (2010). A Federal case for smart design. *Engineered Systems Magazine*. http://www.esmagazine.com

Hasan, Z. M. (2018). *Exploring Leadership Styles of a Government Agency for Organizational Sustainability: A Case Study* (Publication No. 2087780277) [Doctoral dissertation, Northcentral University]. ProQuest Dissertations & Theses Global.

Hatchimonji, D. R.; Linsky, Arielle V., DeMarchena, S., Nayman, S. J., Kim, S., & Elias, M. J. (2018). Building a culture of engagement through participatory feedback processes. *Clearing House: A Journal of Educational Strategies, 9*(1), 59-65. https://doi.org/10.1080/00098655.2017.1386000

Herremans, I. M., Nazari, J. A., & Mahmoudian, F. (2016). Stakeholder relationships, engagement, and sustainability reporting. *Journal of Business Ethics, 138*(3), 417-435. https://doi.org/10.1007/s10551-015-2634-0

Huitt, W. (2007). Maslow's hierarchy of needs. *Educational Psychology Interactive*. Valdosta State University. http://www.edpsycinteractive.org/topics/regsys/maslow.html

Hult, G., Cavusgil, S., Kiyak, T., Deligonul, S., & Lagerström, K. (2007). What drives performance in globally focused marketing organizations?: A three-country study. *Journal of International Marketing, 15*(2), 58-85. https://doi.org/10.1509/jimk.15.2.58

Jamali, D. (2006). Insights into triple bottom line integration from a learning organization perspective. *Business Process Management, 12*(6), 809-821. https://doi.org/10.1108/14637150610710945

Kalbers, L. P. (2009). Fraudulent financial reporting, corporate governance, and ethics: 1987-2007. *Review of Accounting & Finance, 8*(2), 187-209. https://doi.org/10.1108/14757700910959510

Kant, I. (1959). *Foundations of the metaphysics of morals.* Bobbs-Merril.

Kanwar, Y., Singh, A., & Kodwani, A. (2009). Work-life balance and burnout as predictor of job satisfaction in the IT-ITES industry. *Vision (09722629), 13*(2), 1-12. https://doi.org/10.1177/097226290901300201

Kazancoglu. I., Sagnak. M., Mangla. S. K., & Kazancoglu. Y. (2020). Circular economy and the policy: A framework for improving the corporate environmental management in supply chains. *Business Strategy and the Environment, 30*(1), 590-608. https://doi.org/10.1002/bse.2641

Ko, C., Ma, J., Bartnik, R., Haney, M. H., & Kang, M. (2018). Ethical leadership: An integrative review and future research agenda. *Ethics & Behavior, 28*, 104–132. https://doi.org/10.1080/10508422.2017.1318069

Korkmaz, T., & Arpaci, E. (2009). Relationship of organizational citizenship behavior with emotional intelligence. *Procedia Social Behavioral Sciences, 1*, 2432-2435. https://doi.org/10.1016/j.sbspro.2009.01.428

Kooskora, M. (2013). The role of (the right) values in an economic crisis. *Journal of Management & Change, 30/31*(1/2), 49-65.

Laine, M. (2016). Culture sustainability- defining cultural sustainability in education. *Discourse and Communication for Sustainable Education, 7*(2), 52-67. https://doi.org/10.1515/dcse-2016-0016

Larco, N. (2009). Hybridizing place: global and local identity in Puerto Madero, Buenos Aires. *International Planning Studies, 14*(3), 275-292.

Linnenluecke, M. K., & Griffiths, A. (2010). Corporate sustainability and organizational culture. *Journal of World Business, 45*, 357⊠366. https://doi.org/10.1016/j.jwb.2009.08.006

Lorincová, S., Štarcho. P., Weberová. D., Hitka. M., & Lipoldová. M. (2019). Employee motivation as a tool to achieve sustainability of business processes. *Sustainability, 11*, 3509. https://doi.org/10.3390/su11133509

Maharani, D. P. A., & Roshandi, F. N. (2019). Do types of organizational culture correlate with the job satisfaction?: A study on employee's perception. *Journal Administrasi Kesehatan Indonesia, 7*(2), 162-169. https://doi.org/10.20473/jaki.v7i2.2019.162-169

Malik, M. F., & Akhtar, S. (2017). Effect of ambivalence on employee creativity. *Journal of Hotel & Business Management, 6*(2). https://doi.org/10.4172/2169-0286.1000166

Mathur, G., & Dabas, D. (2014). Innovation as a predicator of organizational sustainability in sports industry. *Review of HRM, 3*, 51-66.

Marsh, C. (2013). Business executives' perceptions of ethical leadership and its development. *Journal of Business Ethics, 114*(3), 565-582. https://doi.org/10.1007/s10551-012-1366-7

Mayer, D. M., Kuenzi, M., Greenbaum, R., Bardes, M., & Salvador, R. (2009). How low does ethical leadership flow?: Test of a trickle-down model. *Organizational Behavior & Human Decision Processes, 108*(1), 1-13. https://doi.org/10.1016/j.obhdp.2008.04.002

Mayer, J. D., Caruso, D. R., & Salovey, P. (2016). The ability model of emotional intelligence. Principles and updates. *Emotion Review, 8*, 1-11. https://doi.org/10.1177/1754073916639667

McCann, J. (2004). Organizational effectiveness: changing concepts for changing environments. *Human Resource Planning, 27*(1), 42-50.

McFadzean, E. (1998). The creativity continuum: Towards a classification of creative problem solving techniques. *Creativity and Innovation Management, 7*(3), 131-139. https://doi.org/10.1111/1467-8691.00101

Metcalf, L., & Benn, S. (2013). Leadership for sustainability: An evolution of leadership ability. *Journal of Business Ethics, 112*(3), 369-384. https://doi.org/10.1007/s10551-012-1278-6

Meyer, M. H., Anzani, M., & Walsh, G. (2005). Organizational change for enterprise growth. *Research Technology Management, 48*(6), 48-56.

Modassir, A., & Singh, T. (2008). Relationship of emotional intelligence with transformational leadership and organizational citizenship behavior. *International Journal of Leadership Studies, 4*(1), 3-21. https://doi.org/10.2139/ssrn.2145266

Moktadir, M. A., Dwivedi, A., & Rahman, A. (2020). An investigation of key performance indicators for operational excellence towards sustainability in the leather products industry. *Business Strategy Environment, 29*, 3331–3351. https://doi.org/10.1002/bse.2575

Monga, M. (2016). Integrity and its antecedents: A unified conceptual framework of integrity. *The Journal of Developing Areas, 50*(5), 415-421. https://doi.org/10.1353/jda.2016.0040

Montiel, I., & Delgado-Ceballos, J. (2014). Defining and measuring corporate sustainability: Are we there yet? *Organization &amp Environment, 27*(2), 113-139. https://doi.org/10.1177/108602661452641

Morris, M. (2012). Sustainability: An exercise in futility. *International Journal of Business and Management, 7*(2), 36-44. https://doi.org/10.5539/ijbm. v7n2p36

Morris, M. H., Davis, D. L., & Allene, J. W. (1994). Fostering corporate entrepreneurship: cross-cultural comparisons of the importance of individualism versus collectivism. *Journal of International Business Studies, 25*(1), 65-89. https://doi.org/10.1057/palgrave.jibs.8490849

Motivation. (2003). In The New Penguin Business Dictionary. http://www. credoreference.com/entry/penguinbus/motivation

Motivation. (2006). In business. The Ultimate Resource - Dictionary of Business and Management. Credoreference. http://www.credoreference. com/entry/ultimatebusiness/motivation

National Geographic. (2016). *Air pollution.* National Geographic. https:// www.nationalgeographic.com/environment/global-warming/pollution/

Neera, J., Anjanee, S., & Shoma, M. (2010). Leadership dimensions and challenges in the new millennium. *Advances in Management, 3*(3), 18-24.

Nuno, F. (2020). Economic effects of coronavirus outbreak (C-*-*-*-*-19) on the world economy. http://dx.doi.org/10.2139/ssrn.3557504

Ogbonna, E., & Harris, L. (2016). Leadership style, organizational culture, and performance: Empirical evidence from UK companies. *The International Journal of Human Resources Management, 11*(4), 766-788. https://doi. org/10.1080/09585190050075114

Ojha, S. (2015). Operational excellence for sustainability of Nepalese Industries. *Procedia-Social and Behavioral Sciences, 189*, 458-464. https:// doi/10.1016/j.sbspro.2015.03.196

Ölcer, F., Florescu, M. S., & Nastase, M. (2014). The effects of transformational leadership and emotional intelligence of managers on organizational citizenship behaviors of employees. *Review of International Comparative Management, 15*(4), 385-401.

Opoku, A., Ahmed, V., & Cruickshank, H. (2015). Leadership style of sustainability professionals in the UK construction industry. *Built Environment Project and Asset Management, 5*(2), 184-201. https://doi.org/10.1108/BEP AM-12-2013-0075

Opuni, F. F., & Adu-Gyamfi, K. (2014). An analysis of the impact of emotional intelligence on service quality and customer satisfaction in the telecommunication sector in Ghana. *International Journal of Sales & Marketing Management Research and Development*, 4(3), 11-26.

Perkasa, D. H., & Abadi, F. (2019). The effect of emotional intelligence servant leadership, and organizational commitment on organizational citizenship behavior. *4th International Conference on Management Economics and Business (ICMEB 2019)*.

Prugh, T., & Assadourian, E. (2003). What is sustainability, anyway? *World Watch*, 16(5). http://www.woldwatch.org

Ribeiro, M. M., Hoover, E., Burford, G., Buchebner, J., & Lindenthal, T. (2016). Values as a bridge between sustainability and institutional assessment: A case study from BOKU University. *International Journal of Sustainability in Higher Education*, 17(1), 40-53. https://doi.org/10.1108/IJSHE-12-2014-0170

Romanelli, M. (2018). Organization and people for sustainability *Management Dynamics in the Knowledge Economy*, 6(1), 117128. https://doi.org/10.25019/MDKE/6.1.07

Salovey, P., & Mayer, J. D. (1990). Emotional intelligence. *Imagination, Cognition, and Personality*, 9, 185-211. https://scholars.unh.edu/cgi/viewcontent.cgi?article=1007&context=personality_labhttps://scholars.unh.edu

Schaefer, K., Particia, D. C., & Kearins, K. (2015). Social, environmental and sustainable entrepreneurship research: What is needed for sustainability-as-flourishing? *Organization & Environment*, 28(4), 394-413. https://doi.org/10.1177/1086026615621111

Shahhosseini, M., Silong, A. D., Ismaill, I. A., & Uli, J. (2012). The role of emotional intelligence on job performance. *International Journal of Business and Social Science*, 3(21), 241-246. https://scholars.unh.edu/https://ijbssnet.com/journals

Simons, T., Leroy, H., Collewaert, V., & Masschelein, S. (2015). How leader alignment of words and deeds affects followers: A meta-analysis of behavioral integrity research. *Journal of Business Ethics*, 132(4), 831-844. https://doi.org/10.1007/s10551-014-2332-3

Smith, S. S., Peters, R., & Caldwell, C. (2016). Creating a culture of engagement -- Insights for application. *Business and Management Research*, 5(2), 70-80. https://doi.org/10.5430/bmr.v5n2p70

Stedham. Y., & Skaar. T. B. (2019). Mindfulness, trust, and leader effectiveness: A conceptual framework. *Front. Psychology, 10,* 1588. https://doi.org/10.3389/fpsyg.2019.01588

Stoughton, A. M., & Ludema, J. (2012). The driving forces of sustainability. *Journal of Organizational Change Management, 25*(4), 501-517. https://doi.org/10.1108/09534811211239191

Stuart, J. H. (2013). Positioning the corporate brand as sustainable: Leadership de rigueur. *Journal of Brand Management, 20*(9), 793-799. https://doi.org/10.1057/bm.2013.17

Suriyankietkaew, S. (2013). Emergent leadership paradigms for corporate sustainability: A proposed model. *The Journal of Applied Business Research, 29*(1), 173-182. https://doi.org/10.19030/jabr.v29i1.7565

Swanson, L. A., & Zhang, D. D. (2012). Perspectives on corporate responsibility and sustainable development. *Management of Environmental Quality, 23*(6), 630-639. https://doi.org/10.1108/14777831211262918

Takaku, R., & Yokoyama, I. (2020). *What school closure left in its wake: Contrasting evidence between parents and children from the first C-*-*-*-*-19 outbreak.* http://doi.org/10.2139/ssrn.3693484

U.S. Census Bureau. National Population Totals and Components of Change: 2010-2019. (2019). https://www.census.gov/data/datasets/time-series/demo/popest/2010s-national-total.html

Vanitha, P., Dharanipria, M., & Ramesh, C. (2020). Emotional intelligence and its impact on work performance. *Turkish Journal of Psychology and Rehabilitation, 32*(3), 2964-2970. https://turkjphysiotherrehabill.org/

Veríssimo, J. M. C., & Lacerda, T. M. C. (2015). Does integrity matter for CSR practice in organizations?: The mediating role of transformational leadership. *Business Ethics A European Review, 24*(1), 34-51. https://doi.org/10.1111/beer.12065

Weber, J. (1993). Institutionalizing ethics into business organizations: A model and research agenda. *Business Ethics Quarterly, 3*(4), 419-439. https://doi.org/10.2307/3857287

Wilk, R. (2017). Without consumer culture, there is no environmental crisis. *Cyberseminar on Culture, Beliefs, and the Environment,* 15-19. https://www.populationenvironmentresearch.org/cyberseminars/10449

Winston, V. (2011). Sustainability and social justice. *International Journal of Business and Social Science, 2*(6), 33-37. https://www.semanticscholar.org

Wojtkowiak, D., & Cyplik, P.(2020). Operational excellence within sustainable development concept-systematic literature review. *Sustainability,* 2(19), 7933. https://doi/doi:10.3390/su12197933

Wonglimpiyarat, J. (2012). Technology strategies and standard competition — comparative innovation cases of Apple and Microsoft. *Journal of High Technology Management Research, 23*(2), 90-102. https://doi.org/10.1016/j.hitech.2012.06.005

World Commission on Environment and Development (WCED). (1987). *Our common future.* Oxford University Press.

World Nuclear Association. (2018). *Nuclear power in France.* World-nuclear. http://www.world-nuclear.org/information-library/country-profiles/countries-a-f/france.aspx

Xu, X., Liu, W., & Pang, W. (2019). Are emotionally intelligent people more creative?: A meta-analysis of the emotional-creativity link. *Sustainability.* https://doi.org/10.3390/su11216123

Yallaparagada, R. R. (2007). There is no accounting for Fannie Mae. *Journal of Business & Economics Research, 5*(7), 65-70. https://doi.org/10.19030/jber.v5i7.2563

ABOUT THE AUTHOR

Dr. Zuhair Hasan has more than 24 years in consulting engineering practice and construction and has worked on projects totaling worth of more than $2 billion, where he focuses on sustainability of projects, specifically energy and water savings, renewable energy usage, and sustainability policy formulation. His experience as a project manager and as a consulting engineer includes private sector and public sector organizations. He is an entrepreneur and an independent sustainability leadership consultant and researcher.

Dr. Zuhair Hasan earned his Ph.D. in Business Administration from Northcentral University, a Master's degree in Building Construction from the Georgia Institute of Technology, and a BSc in Mechanical Engineering from Birzeit University. Additionally, he is a frequent author and coauthor of articles on both sustainability in engineering practice and leadership, including *Virtuous Leadership – Insights for the 21st Century, A Federal Case for Smart Design, and 5 Proven Methods That Will Make You the Leader People Admire.*

Dr. Zuhair Hasan can be reached at his email address at: Dr.ZuhairHasan@gmail.com

INDEX

www.ingramcontent.com/pod-product-compliance
Lightning Source LLC
Chambersburg PA
CBHW060318030426
42336CB00011B/1111